Sally Burgess with Richard Acklam and Araminta Crace

going for Gold

Intermediate

language maximiser

Longman

Contents

Introduction to the *language maximiser* p. 4

Reading	Writing	Listening	Speaking
True/False questions	Spelling and punctuation		Talking about likes and dislikes
	Informal letters	Multiple choice	
True/False questions	Paragraphs		Describing a photograph
	Story	Multiple choice	
	Story		Giving opinions; Agreeing and disagreeing
Multiple choice	Notes and messages	True/False questions	
	Informal letters and punctuation	Completing notes	Helping your partner contribute to the discussion
Multiple choice	Transactional letter and linkers of contrast		
Multiple matching	Discursive composition		Comparing two photographs
	Report	Extracts	Coming to a decision
Multiple choice	Informal letters		
Gapped text	Story	Extracts	Describing a photograph
	Article	Completing notes	
Multiple matching	Transactional letter		Pausing before speaking and asking someone's opinion
	Report	Extracts	Review

Introduction to the *going for Gold language maximiser*

What is the *language maximiser*?

The *language maximiser* is designed to give you plenty of practice of the grammar and vocabulary presented in *going for Gold* Coursebook, plus extra reading, listening, writing and speaking practice.

What is in each unit?

Each unit contains two **Grammar** sections. In these sections you will find an *About the language* box with the most important grammar, as well as 'typical mistakes' that many students make. These mistakes have been corrected for you so that you know how to avoid them in your own work. Of course, there are plenty of exercises that will help you learn these grammar points and have fun at the same time!

All the units have **Vocabulary** sections as well. These practise the words and expressions you studied in *going for Gold* Coursebook, but you will also learn some new words and expressions from the same topic area. There is plenty of practice, including crosswords and other puzzles, as well as extra help with recording and learning vocabulary.

There is either a **Reading** or a **Listening** section in every unit too. These provide more practice with the kinds of reading and listening tasks you saw in *going for Gold* Coursebook. Most units have a **Speaking** section where you can listen to other people talking and learn how to take part in a conversation in English yourself.

Writing is very important, so we have made sure that you get lots of writing practice. There is a **Writing** section in every unit of the *language maximiser*. In these sections you will often see this symbol ⚡ . Next to it you will find important information that you should study carefully. You will be able to see examples of other people's writing and learn how to improve your own formal and informal letters, stories, notes and messages, compositions, articles and reports.

How can I use the *language maximiser*?

You can use the *language maximiser* with your teacher or on your own. Most of the time you will write your answers to the exercises in the *language maximiser* itself. Almost all the questions have only one answer so they are very easy to correct. If you have a *language maximiser* with a key, you can do the exercises at home and correct them yourself. If you have a *language maximiser* without a key, then your teacher will correct them or go through them with you in class.

You can use the *language maximiser* to check that you have learnt the grammar and vocabulary in each unit of the *going for Gold* Coursebook or to revise for tests and exams. All the Grammar sections in the *language maximiser* tell you on which page in the Coursebook you studied that particular grammar point. The Writing sections tell you where to look in the Writing Reference in the Coursebook too, so it is very easy to revise. You can also use the *language maximiser* to check your progress with listening, speaking, reading and writing.

We hope you learn a lot and have fun using *going for Gold* Language Maximiser.

A question of family

Grammar 1: Questions ▶ *CB page 6*

About the language

Yes/No questions

- With *be, have got, may, can, could, would, should*:

  He **has** got two sisters.

  Has he got two sisters? Yes, he has.

- With other verbs:

  He **misses** his home town.

  Does he miss his home town? No, he doesn't.

Wh- questions

Wh- question word	+	auxiliary	+	subject	+	main verb

Where	do	your cousins	live?
Why	are	you	learning English?
Where	does	he	work?
Who	is	that boy?	
When	does	the class	begin?
How long	have	you	been learning English?
What	is	your name?	

- Questions about the subject don't use *do/does/did*.

  Tom likes dogs.

  Object question: *What **does** Tom like?*   *Dogs.*
  Subject question: *Who likes dogs?*   *Tom.*

- Prepositions (*at, by, for, from, in, like, on, to, with* etc.) usually go after the main verb.

  *Which member of your family do you have most respect **for**?*

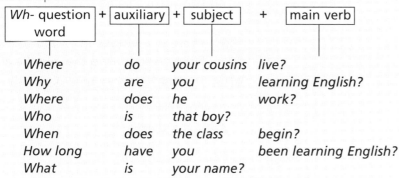

Typical mistakes

Do you miss
~~Miss you~~ your family?

          does
Where ^ your sister live?

     does   *live*
Where ~~live~~ your sister ^ ?

1 Write *yes/no* questions for these statements.

0 He is Spanish.

   Is he Spanish? ....

1 He is in our class.

....

2 He lives near the school.

....

3 He has got a sister called Claudia.

....

4 He plays football for the school team.

....

5 He has got a motorbike.

....

6 I am meeting him after school today.

....

2   Complete these questions with appropriate question words.

0 ....._Who_..... is your best friend?

1 .... does she live?

2 .... does she spend her free time?

3 .... is her favourite subject at school?

4 .... brothers and sisters does she have?

5 .... is she closest to in her family?

6 .... is she learning English?

7 .... does she look like?

3   Put the words in order to make questions.

0 surname what your is

   What is your surname?

1 spell how you name your do

2 living you are where moment at the

3 do do you what

4 many how brothers and sisters got have you

5 cinema how often go you do to the

6 did last you when go out with friends

7 English learning long how you have been

8 learning why English you are

9 a film much cost it does to see in your how city

10 to visit country which most like would you

11 one of your favourite who singers is

12 advice listen to whose often most you do

4   Match these answers to the questions in exercise 3.

a) It's Braun.   _0_

b) K – A – T – E – R – I – N – A.   _ _

c) Shakira. But only when she sings
    in Spanish.   _ _

d) With my parents in a small city in
    the north of my country.   _ _

e) One brother. He's two years older
    than me.   _ _

f) On Saturday. We went to the movies
    and then for a pizza.   _ _

g) Australia. I'd really like to see
    the animals.   _ _

h) Because it's important for my future.   _ _

i) About three Euros.   _ _

j) About three years.   _ _

k) I'm a student.   _ _

l) My aunt's. She's really wise.   _ _

m) About twice a month.   _ _

5   There is a mistake in each of the following questions. Find the mistake and write the questions out again correctly.

0 You are a teacher?

   Are you a teacher?

1 What subject teach you?

2 Where you work?

3 Does you enjoy your job?

4 How many students have you?

5 Is you married?

6 Who does get out of bed first in your house?

Grammar 2: Indirect questions ▶ *CB page 9*

About the language

- All indirect questions follow the same word order as statements (subject + verb).

subject		verb

  *What **is** your name?* ▶ *Could you tell me what **your name** **is**?*

- In indirect *wh*-questions we don't use *do, does* or *did*.
  *Where **do you live** ▶ Could you tell me where **you live**?*

- Indirect *Yes/No* questions use *if* or *whether*.
  ***Do you enjoy** learning languages?*

  ▼

  *Would you mind telling me **if you enjoy** learning languages?*

- If the indirect question does not begin with a question we don't use a question mark (?) at the end.
  I'd like to know if you feel closer to your brother or your sister.

> **Typical mistakes** •
>
> *I'd like to know why are you studying English.*
> *Could you tell me how many brothers and sisters you do have?*
> *Could you tell me how many brothers and sisters do you have?*
>   *if/whether*
> *I'd like to know do you enjoy studying English.*
> *Could you to tell me where the post office is?*
> *Can you tell me where the dictionaries are?*

1   Choose the correct alternative to complete these indirect questions.

0 Can you tell me …
  A … where is the post office? ☐
  B … where the post office is? ☑

1 I'd like to know …
  A … what her name is. ☐
  B … what is her name. ☐

2 Could you tell me …
  A … if there is a bank near here? ☐
  B … is there a bank near here? ☐

3 I'd like to know …
  A … where you live? ☐
  B … where you live. ☐

4 I'd like to know …
  A … did you arrive on time. ☐
  B … whether you arrived on time. ☐

5 Could you tell me …
  A … if you like swimming? ☐
  B … if you like swimming. ☐

2   Write indirect questions from these prompts.

0 how / feel / about learning English
  I'd like to know *how you feel about learning English.*

1 when / start / learning English
  Could you tell me ....

  ....

2 enjoy / first English class
  I'd like to know ....

  ....

3 what / name / of your English book
  Could you tell me ....

  ....

4 coming / to class tomorrow
  I'd like to know ....

  ....

5 like / playing football
  Could you tell me ....

  ....

3   Change the questions on the notepad into indirect questions and put them into the conversation below.

0 What's your full name?

1 How do you spell your surname?

2 Where do you live?

3 Do you live alone?

4 How many of you live at that address?

5 Are you studying or working?

6 How much do you spend on entertainment each week?

7 What kinds of entertainment do you enjoy most?

A: Could you tell me (0) ___*what your full name is?*___

B: Enrique Wolfson.

A: Could you tell me (1)..

....

B: W-O-L-F-S-O-N

A: Thank you. Could you tell me (2)..............................

....

B: 15 Dawson Street, Clifton Gardens.

A: I'd like to know (3)..

....

B: No, I share the house with friends.

A: Could you tell me (4) ....

....

B: There are three of us sharing at the moment.

A: I'd like to know (5)..

....

B: We've all got part-time jobs but we're studying together at the college.

A: Could you tell me (6) ....

....

B: About twenty-five pounds.

A: Could you tell me (7) ....

....

B: The cinema, going out for meals with friends and listening to music.

Reading

1   Josh (Joshua) Jackson is one of the young actors in a famous television series called *Dawson's Creek*. Read this interview from a movie magazine. Match the places to the things Josh says about them.

A Europe   D Ireland
B Canada   E Vancouver
C California

0 His grandparents lived there.   *D*
1 He and his family lived there for a while.   ....
2 He likes this place very much.   ....
3 He was born there and he lives there now.   ....
4 He wants to go and study there.   ....

A Rising Star

Teen Movie Mag: Where did you grow up?

Josh: In Vancouver, Canada. We lived in California for a while but we moved back to Canada when I was nine.

TMM: When did you start acting?

Josh: Just after we moved back to Canada. I did some television advertisements and then I got a [1]part in a TV series.

TMM: Did you know that *Dawson's Creek* would go on for so long when you [2]auditioned for the role of Pacey Witter?

Josh: No way! I was just really [3]delighted to have a chance to work as an actor. I'm [4]amazed that it's been such a huge success!

TMM: Are any other members of your family actors?

2   Look at these statements. Read the text and circle the part of the interview that tells you if each statement is correct or incorrect. If it is correct, put a ✓. If it is not correct, put a ✗.

0   Josh is from California.   ✗

1   He has been acting since he was a child.   _

2   He knew *Dawson's Creek* would be a success.   _

3   His grandparents lived in Ireland.   _

4   He wants to go to university in North America.   _

5   He likes his home town very much.   _

6   He doesn't like to be alone.   _

7   He is always very busy.   _

Josh: My sister acts too and both my grandparents were opera singers in Ireland so I suppose it runs in the family.

TMM: You didn't go to university after you left school. Would you still like to go?

Josh: Yes, I would. But I'd like to study somewhere in Europe. I've always lived in North America and I think a change would be good.

TMM: What are ten things you couldn't live without?

Josh: Family (especially my mother and my sister), friends (I've got friends everywhere), my home town, Vancouver (it's a fantastic city), my dog Shumba (his name means *lion* in Swahili), camping, nature, being on my own, acting, learning and kiwi fruit. They're ⁵scrumptious!

TMM: You seem to be very busy. Do you have time for a personal life?

Josh: It depends. Sometimes life is really ⁶hectic and I don't have a moment for myself. Other times it's not so bad. We film during the day and then I go home at night just like someone with a normal nine-to-five job.

Vocabulary: Working out meaning from context ▶ *CB page 5*

1   Here are some things other students do when they find words that they don't understand in a text. Match what the students do to the comments 1–4 below. Write the student's name on the line.

I continue reading and try not to worry about the words I don't understand.

Rafaella

Stefan

I look all the words up in a dictionary.

Claudia

I look up important words in my dictionary.

David

I try and work out the meaning of important words from the context.

1 ....   2 ....

This doesn't work. Some words are not important and it takes much too long to read the text!

This is a very good idea. When you work out the meaning from context you usually remember the new word better.

3 ....

This is not such a good idea. You might not understand anything at all!

4 ....

This can be very useful but I only do it when I've already tried to work out what the word means from context.

2   There are two steps in working out the meaning of a word from context:

• First decide on the part of speech (noun, verb, adjective etc.) of the word.

• Then look at the words and sentences before and after the word.

Look at the nonsense words in *italics* in these sentences and decide what they mean. <u>Underline</u> the words that help you decide, as in the example.

0   A <u>bright red</u> *gimble* came round the corner very fast and almost <u>knocked me down</u>. <u>The driver</u> didn't even see me.

    A *gimble* is: Ⓐ a type of car

                       B a type of animal

1   She *nordled* all her final exams because she hadn't studied at all.

    To *nordle* means: A to sing   B to fail

2   He was wearing jeans, a t-shirt and a pair of *galvies*.

    Galvies are: A shoes   B books

3   Francesca is a very *snorpy* person. Terrible things are always happening to her.

    Snorpy means: A unlucky   B lucky

4   She *toogled* into the classroom and told everyone the news.

    To *toogle* means: A to smile   B to run

3   Look at the <u>underlined</u> words in the interview with Josh Jackson on pages 8 and 9 and decide what part of speech they are. Write *noun*, *verb*, or *adjective* in column A.

	A	B
1	....	....
2	....	....
3	....	....
4	....	....
5	....	....
6	....	....

4   Look at the words and sentences before and after the <u>underlined</u> words. Now decide which of the words or phrases in the box below has the closest meaning. Write that word or phrase in column B above.

> busy   surprised   acting job   delicious
> did an acting test   pleased

Speaking ▶ *CB page 8*

1   🖭 Listen to two students, Donatella and Mario, doing *going for Gold* Coursebook Speaking exercise 4 on page 8. Put a tick (✓) next to the things they like doing with their families and a cross (✗) next to the things they don't like doing.

		Mario	Donatella
family holidays	🧳	......✓......	....
watching TV	⬭	....	....
family celebrations	🎂	....	....
shopping	🎁	....	....
going to museums and art galleries	🖼	....	....

2   🖭 Listen again and complete the questions Donatella and Mario ask each other.

1   .... going on holiday with your family?

2   .... you?

3   .... going to museums and art galleries? .... doing that kind of thing with your family?

3   🖭 Listen again and complete these expressions that Donatella and Mario use to say what they like and dislike.

1   I .... that but I .... to go camping or to music festivals with friends too.

2   I .... family holidays.

3   I prefer listening to music and I .... playing it too.

4   I .... shopping. Especially with my sister Gloria.

Writing: Spelling and punctuation

▶ *Writing Reference pages 148 and 151*

1 Look at these extracts from other students' compositions. There is a spelling mistake in each extract. Find the mistake and correct it.

1 Tina was lieing on her bed listening to music, when she heard a very loud noise.

2 I like makeing my own clothes. I learnt to sew when I was quite young and I still enjoy it a lot.

3 I think it is easier to learn a language if you go to live in the country where they speak that language.

4 The lights went out. It was very dark in the room. She looked in the desk drawer but she couldn't find any matchs.

5 When my little brothers were babys they were really cute. They both had curly blond hair and big green eyes.

6 She was very hungry but she was afraid to ask if she could have another peace of toast.

7 I like studying foreing languages. I hope to work as a translator when I finish university.

8 She opened the cuboard and saw the monster. She screamed but nobody heard her.

2 Here are some sentences from a letter a student wrote. Put in the punctuation. The first one has been done for you as an example.

0 my two brothers are called alex and tony

   My two brothers are called Alex and Tony.

1 weve also got a lot of pets

2 there are three goldfish a canary two cats and a dog

3 the dog who is called jasper is white with one black ear

4 weve had him for about three years now

5 after I finish my exams im going on a long holiday with my friends

6 were going to travel through spain and stay at my uncles house in barcelona

3 Here is the first part of a summary of the rest of the BFG story, which you read on page 10 of the *going for Gold* Coursebook. There is a spelling mistake in each sentence. Find the spelling mistakes and correct them.

The Big Friendly Giant's great big hand came threw the window and took *through* Sophie out of her bed. She was really terrifyd because she thought he was going to eat her. In fact he was takeing her to Giant Land. He had a special job in Giant Land – makking happy dreams for children.

4 Here is the second part of the summary. Put in the punctuation.

the big friendly giant was very different to the other giants in giant land he didnt eat children and all the other giants did he wasnt nearly as big as the other giants either they were all much taller and much uglier however the most important difference was that the big friendly giant loved children he wanted to save them from the bad giants he and sophie went to tell the queen of england about the bad giants sophie and the big friendly giant showed the queens soldiers the way to giant land when they got there they captured the bad giants and sophie and the big friendly giant lived happily ever after

Time out

Grammar 1: Present simple ▶ *CB page 13*

About the language

Present simple

We use the **present simple**

- to talk about **routine or regular repeated actions** (often with **adverbs of frequency** like: *always, often, sometimes* and *never*).

  *I **always get up** early on weekdays.*
  *My brother **doesn't usually ride** his motorbike to university.*

  A: ***Do** you **always have** breakfast?*
  B: *Yes, I do.*

  A: ***Does** Tina **give** you a lift to college **every day**?*
  B: *No, she doesn't. I get the bus on Fridays.*

- to talk about permanent situations.
  *I **live** with my parents.*

1 Complete these statements about permanent situations with verbs from the box. Decide if each statement is true (T) or false (F).

cause   make   ~~freeze~~   keep   eat   boil
speak   enjoy   make

0 Water *freezes* at 0°C.   [T]

1 Bees .... honey.   ☐

2 Water .... at 100°C.   ☐

3 Cars .... our cities clean and quiet.   ☐

4 Cats .... swimming.   ☐

5 People in Switzerland .... French, Russian
   and Italian.   ☐

6 Smoking .... cancer.   ☐

7 Eating lettuce .... you fat.   ☐

8 Dolphins .... fish.   ☐

! Typical mistakes

> *usually go*
> I ~~go usually~~ to the beach at the weekends.
> Do you (every Friday) play badminton?
> A: Do your friends like jazz too?
> *do*
> B: Yes, they ~~like~~.

2 Put the adverbs of frequency in the correct position in these sentences.

0 Sophie goes to the gym on Tuesday evening. (always)

   Sophie always goes to the gym on
   Tuesday evening.

1 She uses the exercise machines and she has a sauna afterwards. (normally/sometimes)

   ....
   ....

2 This means she gets home before ten o'clock. (hardly ever)

   ....
   ....

3 On week nights, she doesn't go to bed any later than eleven o'clock. (usually)

   ....
   ....

4 Of course, at the weekend she doesn't go to bed that early. (ever)

   ....
   ....

5 She goes out dancing, and she dances all night! (often/sometimes)

   ....
   ....

3   Use the prompts to write the complete conversation between two people who have just met at a club.

Adam: (0) You / seem / familiar.

You seem familiar.

....

(1) I / know / you from somewhere?

....

Sophie: Yes. (2) I / study / at the same college as you.

....

(3) you / come / here often?

....

Adam: Well, (4) sometimes / come / here / Saturdays,

....

but (5) not / like / the music very much.

....

(6) you / like / it?

....

Sophie: Not much. (7) prefer / Latin music, actually.

....

Adam: (8) you / speak / Spanish?

....

Sophie: No, (9) not / speak / it

....

but (10) understand / quite a lot.

....

Adam: (11) What / Yo quiero bailar toda la noche / mean?

....

Sophie: I'm not sure but I think (12) it / mean / I / want / to dance all night!

....

4   Read this interview with a celebrity and then complete the article on the right.

Interviewer:	How often do you stay at home and watch TV?
Max:	Never. I go out to clubs every night.
I:	What time do you get home?
Max:	Never before five and often much later!
I:	Do you sleep all day?
Max:	Hardly ever. I don't need much sleep.
I:	So what time do you get up?
Max:	Most days, around midday.
I:	So I don't suppose you have breakfast.
Max:	Yes, I always do.
I:	And do you go to the studio to record in the afternoons?
Max:	Usually.
I:	Do you let journalists ask you questions about your personal life?
Max:	Not often.
I:	Will you let me ask you one?
Max:	OK.
I:	Do you still see Ella Valdere?
Max:	Hardly ever, no.

Like most celebrities, Max has a rather hectic social life. He (0) *never stays* at home and watches TV like the rest of us, instead he goes out to clubs. He doesn't get much sleep either because he (1) .... before five and it (2) .... much later than that. And what time do you think he gets up? Well, you'll be surprised to learn that he (3) .... all day. In fact he (4) .... at about midday and then he (5) .... breakfast. In the afternoon he (6) .... to the studio to record. I managed to ask Max one question about his private life even though he (7) .... let journalists ask him personal questions. I wanted to know if he still sees Ella Valdere. He says he (8) .... her now.

Grammar 2: Present continuous v. present simple ▶ *CB page 18*

About the language

Present continuous

We use the **present continuous**

* to talk about **actions happening now.**

   Take your umbrella. It**'s raining**.

   A: What **are** you **doing** in there?

   B: I**'m having** a shower!

* to talk about **future arrangements**.

   A: What **are** you **doing** tomorrow?

   B: Well, I**'m picking** Ania up at 8.30 and then we**'re going** to a meeting. After that I**'m having** lunch with Simon and then I**'m going** to the dentist.

We **do not** normally use the following verbs in continuous tenses: *hate, know, like, love, mean, need, prefer, seem, understand, want.*

I**'m playing** tennis tomorrow. I **love** tennis, but my brother **hates** it.

We use some verbs in the **present simple** and **present continuous** with different meanings:

think
I **think** Brazil will win the World Cup. (= believe)
I**'m thinking** of buying a digital camera. (= use your mind)

have
Do you **have** any books by Stephen King? (= own)
I **haven't got** many summer clothes. (= own)
We**'re having** a fantastic time here in Rome. (= experience)

see
I **see** what you mean but I don't agree. (= understand)
I**'m seeing** the doctor on Thursday afternoon. (= visit)

Typical mistakes

'm going
This summer I ~~go~~ to England.

don't understand
I ~~am not understanding~~ French very well.

I see
~~I'm seeing~~ what you mean, but I don't agree.

1 Complete this conversation using either the present simple or the present continuous form of the verbs in brackets.

Tony: Hi Sonia. What (0) **are** you **doing** (do)?

Sonia: I (1) .... (try) to fix the video recorder. It (2) .... (not seem) to be working.

Tony: (3) .... (you know) what's wrong with it?

Sonia: I (4) .... (think) there is something stuck inside it.

Tony: (5) .... (you want) me to help you?

Sonia: No thanks. Where's Sophie, by the way?

Tony: She's just outside. We met Adam on the way home from college and she (6) .... (talk) to him in the street. Have you fixed the video yet?

Sonia: Why (7) .... (it worry) you so much?

Tony: Well, it's Tuesday and I (8) .... (go) to basketball practice on Tuesday but my favourite programme is on TV. I (9) .... (always record) it and (10) .... (watch) it when I get home.

2 Underline the correct tense, present simple or present continuous.

0 *Do you think/Are you thinking* it will be sunny at the weekend?

1 *Do you like/Are you liking* pizza?

2 *They think of/They are thinking of* going to Italy this summer.

3 *She seems/She is seeming* familiar.

4 *Do you see/Are you seeing* Mary this weekend? Could you give her a message from me?

5 *Do you see/Are you seeing* what I mean?

6 *I understand/I'm understanding* how you feel.

7 *I have/I'm having* a lot of fun with my new computer at the moment.

8 A: *Are you doing/Do you do* anything special this weekend?

   B: *I'm having/I've got* an exam on Saturday morning, but after that I'm free.

Vocabulary: Free time activities ▶ *CB page 14*

1 Complete these quiz questions about free time activities with verbs from the box.

> collect   go to   play   go   take

ARE YOU A BORING 'COUCH POTATO'?
Answer our quiz on free time activities to find out

1 *How many sports do you .... regularly?*
- **A** None. ☐
- **B** One. ☐
- **C** Two or more. ☐

2 *How often do you .... jogging?*
- **A** Never. ☐
- **B** Once a week. ☐
- **C** More than twice a week. ☐

3 *How often do you .... the stadium to watch your team?*
- **A** Never. ☐
- **B** Once or twice a year. ☐
- **C** Every two weeks. ☐

4 *How many musical instruments do you ....?*
- **A** None. ☐
- **B** One. ☐
- **C** Two or more. ☐

5 *On your last holiday, how many photographs did you ....?*
- **A** None. ☐
- **B** Thirty-six. ☐
- **C** More than one hundred. ☐

6 *Do you .... anything like stamps or records?*
- **A** No. ☐
- **B** Stamps. ☐
- **C** Stamps, records, photos, phonecards, toy cars and newspapers. ☐

7 *How many card games do you know how to ....?*
- **A** None. ☐
- **B** One or two. ☐
- **C** Lots. ☐

8 *What is your idea of a perfect Saturday afternoon?*
- **A** Staying at home and watching TV. ☐
- **B** .... the cinema. ☐
- **C** .... football with friends. ☐

2 Now answer the questions and look at the key on page 110.

3 Read this extract from a letter and choose the correct word for each space. Circle your answer.

My boyfriend Jonathan (0) .... a lot of different things in his free time too. He (1) .... football with friends at the beach in the summer but he is also a member of a team. He (2) .... the football stadium for a training session on Wednesday evenings. The coach usually starts by telling them all to (3) .... jogging for half an hour. Then they come back, do some other exercises and sometimes even (4) .... a practice match against another team. Apart from football, Jonathan also (5) .... tennis and volleyball, but he is not just interested in sports. He (6) .... the guitar with a group too. He loves music from the 1960s and he (7) .... records. He's got more than two hundred records already. When famous groups come to our town we always (8) .... the concerts, especially if they are old groups like the Rolling Stones.

0 Ⓐ does   B makes   C plays

1 A goes   B goes to   C plays

2 A plays   B goes   C goes to

3 A play   B take   C go

4 A take   B play   C go

5 A collects B goes   C plays

6 A takes   B plays   C goes

7 A collects B takes   C goes to

8 A go to   B take   C go

Learner training: Recording vocabulary

1   There are many different ways of recording vocabulary. Look at how a student has recorded some vocabulary about free time activities.

a
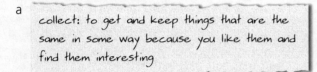
collect: to get and keep things that are the same in some way because you like them and find them interesting

b
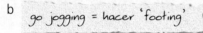
go jogging = hacer 'footing'

c

chess =

d

Verb	Nouns
go	jogging, running, skiing, swimming, shopping
go to	the cinema, an exhibition, a concert, a museum, a music festival, a party
collect	stamps, records, phone cards, tea pots, newspapers
play	sports a musical instrument tennis the guitar baseball the piano ice hockey the saxophone

e
training / ˈtreɪnɪŋ / (noun)
Special physical exercises that are part of a health or fitness plan.
I do circuit training twice a week.

f
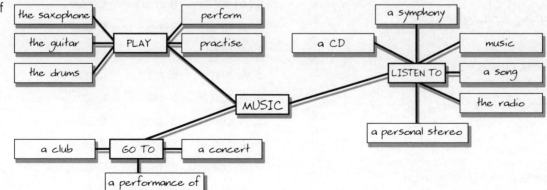

2   Now match the notebook entries to these comments. Write your answers below.

1   This is probably the quickest method, but sometimes it's hard to find a good translation.

2   Grids like this are good for collocation – words that go together. They help you organise the vocabulary you want to learn.

3   I think mind maps are fantastic! You can add more and more words and phrases as you learn them. You can organise new words and phrases so that you remember the connections between them.

4   Writing a short English–English explanation is a useful system because you can practise your English!

5   Drawing pictures like this helps you to remember the word. It's fun too. You can make your Vocabulary Notebook a work of art!

6   It's good to use dictionary entries because you get a lot of information about the word: pronunciation, the meaning and often some examples

1 ......   2 ......   3 ......   4 ......   5 ......   6 ......

Listening

1 📼 You will hear a recording about a zoo and park on the island of Tenerife. Look at this map and tick (✓) the sections in the Key that you hear about on the recording.

Key

1. *Thai village*
2. *Gorillas*
3. *Planet penguin*
4. *Sea lions*
5. *Chimpland*
6. *Cinema*
7. *Alligators*
8. *Orchid garden*
9. *Jaguars*
10. *Parrot show*
11. *Tiger island*
12. *Dolphinarium*
13. *Parrots*
14. *Aquarium – sharks*
15. *Porcelain museum*
☺ *Children's playground*

LORO PARQUE

2 📼 Listen again and put a tick (✓) in the correct box for each question.

1 When does the park open?
   A ten o'clock in the morning ☐
   B eight o'clock in the morning ☐
   C eight o'clock in the evening ☐

2 How long does it take to get to the park by train?
   A ten minutes ☐
   B fifteen minutes ☐
   C twenty minutes ☐

3 When was the film *Nature Rediscovered* first shown?
   A in 2002 ☐
   B in 1992 ☐
   C in 1972 ☐

4 What time is the last parrot show?
   A at 3.30 ☐
   B at 10.30 ☐
   C at 5.30 ☐

5 How many dolphin shows are there every day?
   A two ☐
   B four ☐
   C twelve ☐

6 What can you eat in the restaurant?
   A hamburgers and chips ☐
   B meat, fish and pizza ☐
   C salads ☐

Writing: Informal letters ▶ *Writing Reference page 149*

> ⚡ **Topic sentences**
> Paragraphs often begin with topic sentences. Topic sentences tell you what the paragraph is about. All the other sentences in that paragraph are about the same topic.

1   Read this letter. The topic sentence of each paragraph is missing. Decide what each paragraph is about and then choose the best alternative below. Circle your answer.

Dear Greta

(0) .... My cousin Francesca and her boyfriend have been to visit me on holiday.

(1) .... In the morning we looked at the shops and visited the cathedral. After lunch we went to the historical museum and then walked along the river. I think they both enjoyed the day.

(2) .... The last time we were together was about four years ago, but she hasn't changed much at all. She still has the same wonderful smile and sense of humour.

Do write back soon and let me know all your news.

Love

Philippa

---

0 A Thanks for your letter.
  Ⓑ Sorry not to have written sooner but I've been very busy.
  C How are you? I am fine.

1 A Francesca really enjoys shopping, as you know.
  B We spent last Saturday showing them around the town.
  C Francesca's boyfriend likes taking photographs.

2 A It was really lovely to see Francesca again.
  B Francesca met her boyfriend in London.
  C Francesca wants to study photography.

2   Now look at these topic sentences and decide which of the sentences (A–C) could not come next. Circle the incorrect sentence.

1 I saw a really good film on TV last Friday.
  A It is a new wide screen TV with a stereo sound system.
  B It was called *The Red Squirrel* and it starred Emma Suárez.
  C I can't remember what it was called but Ben Affleck, who is one of my favourite actors, was in it.

2 It was a thriller.
  A At the beginning a girl has a motorcycle accident and loses her memory completely.
  B My brother was studying for a maths test in his bedroom and kept asking me to turn the TV down.
  C The main character seems like a really good person at the beginning, but he is hiding a terrible secret.

3 By the way, have you heard what happened to Sandro?
  A He was walking home from college one day last week and he fell and broke his ankle.
  B It was at 10 a.m. on the 17th September in the Piazza Navona.
  C You know how unlucky he is. Well, a few weeks ago someone stole his wallet while he was waiting for a train.

4 He's still quite depressed about it, actually.
  A We've all been trying to cheer him up by going round to visit him.
  B Apparently, the wallet had quite a lot of money in it as well as his identity card and a photo of his girlfriend.
  C I don't like being with people who are always complaining and looking sad.

Grammar 1: Gerunds ▶ CB page 21

About the language

Gerunds

- We use **gerunds** when we are talking about an action or activity which is the subject of the sentence.

  Swimming *is one of my favourite activities.*

- We use **gerunds** when the verb is immediately after a preposition.

  I'm looking forward **to seeing** *you.*
  We thought **of buying** *her some perfume.*

Typical mistakes

of waiting
I'm tired ~~to wait~~ for the bus.

taking
I'm nervous about ~~take~~ the exam.

of
She was afraid ~~for~~ flying.

1 Complete these sentences about the signs on the right.

1 .... is not allowed inside the building.

2 .... your dog into the supermarket with you is not allowed.

3 .... your trolley on the escalator is not allowed.

4 .... your mobile phone or laptop computer switched on is dangerous.

5 .... and .... in the library have been banned.

6 .... photos during the concert is not allowed.

2 Complete the second sentence so that it is similar in meaning to the first sentence. Start each sentence with a gerund.

0 I feel confident when I wear yellow.
   Wearing yellow makes me feel confident.

1 I feel anxious when I go for job interviews.

   ....

2 I feel lazy when I get up late.

   ....

3 I feel stronger if I take vitamin tablets.

   ....

4 I feel more relaxed if I get enough sleep.

   ....

5 I seem aggressive if I shout loudly at other people.

   ....

6 I feel unhealthy if I eat a lot of fat and sugar.

   ....

1   2

3   4

5   6

3   Match the sentence beginnings to the sentence endings.

1 I'm tired …

2 My sister is really good …

3 I'm looking forward …

4 They apologised …

5 Are you interested …

a) in making new friends and improving your English? ☐

b) of watching these boring old shows on TV. Let's go out! ☐

c) for making so much noise. ☐

d) at fixing machines. ☐

e) to going on holiday. ☐

4   Complete these sentences with prepositions from the box. Some prepositions can be used more than once.

without	for	of	to	before	about

1 .... going out in the sun, use some sunscreen.

2 Do you have a special place .... keeping old letters?

3 One way .... make a good impression is to wear the right colours.

4 There's no need to be nervous .... meeting my parents. They're very easy-going.

5 I closed the door .... realising I didn't have the key.

6 Instead .... going by train we decided to walk.

7 What's your excuse .... arriving so late?

8 I thought .... going to Australia for Christmas but I decided not to.

9 .... thinking, I told Nieves about the surprise party.

10 I always listen to the weather forecast .... deciding what to wear.

Grammar 2: Gerunds and infinitives ▶
CB page 25

About the language

Gerunds and infinitives

Verb + gerund

Some verbs are followed by a gerund.

*I **enjoy travelling** and **meeting** people from other countries.*

Here are some of the verbs that are followed by a gerund:

enjoy, imagine, suggest, avoid, involve, consider, finish.

Verb + infinitive

Some verbs are followed by an infinitive. We use many of these verbs to talk about things we will do in the future.

*I **hope to visit** Ireland next summer.*

Here are some verbs that are followed by an infinitive:

decide, plan, agree, offer, arrange, hope, manage.

! Typical mistakes ....

He suggested ~~to~~ going by car.

*   to
We decided ∧go to the beach in the afternoon.*

1   There are mistakes in seven of these sentences. Find the mistakes and correct them.

1 I really enjoy to cook.

2 When I'm older, I hope to become a chef.

3 I'm considering to go to Paris to study at a famous cooking school.

4 I could only go if I manage improving my French.

5 A friend suggested to going to a language school.

6 But I've decided not to do this.

7 I've got some friends who speak French and they've offered to teach me.

8 I've agreed teaching them Italian in exchange.

9 We've arranged to meet for our first class next week.

10 We plan spend half the time on French and the other half on Italian.

11 I imagine myself speaking perfect French in a couple of months.

12 When I finish to study, I always cook myself a delicious meal.

2 Complete these sentences with a gerund or an infinitive with *to*. Use the verbs in the box.

> kill   learn   have   ~~watch~~   wash   help
> spend   visit   speak   leave   drive

0 Do you enjoy *watching* films on DVD or video more than going to the cinema?

1 I've decided not .... a holiday this year. I haven't got enough money.

2 Haven't you finished .... those dishes yet?

3 You promised never .... me.

4 If you manage .... to Terry, say 'hi' to him from me.

5 Would you mind .... me with this suitcase? It's very heavy.

6 I always try to avoid .... insects if I can.

7 Starting a new job usually involves .... a few weeks getting used to everything.

8 Which cities do you plan .... while you are in Italy?

9 Tina's brother offered .... me to the airport.

10 Have you ever considered .... another foreign language?

Vocabulary: Word formation ▶
CB page 22

1 Use the *suffixes* (letters you add to the end of a word) in the boxes to change these verbs and adjectives into nouns.

> -ment   -ation   -ion

verb	noun
0 announce	*announcement*
1 inform	....
2 impress	....
3 improve	....
4 enjoy	....
5 alter	....
6 excite	....

> -ness   -ity

adjective	noun
7 weak	....
8 secure	....
9 flexible	....
10 lazy	....

2 Now use the nouns to complete the texts on this and the next page.

> **Public (0)** *Announcement*
> Old notes and coins can be exchanged for Euros until 30th June, 2004.

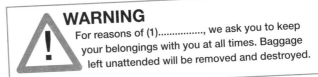

WARNING
For reasons of (1)................, we ask you to keep your belongings with you at all times. Baggage left unattended will be removed and destroyed.

> **APOLOGY**
> We are making some (2)................
> to the building which we are sure
> will be an (3)................ .
> We apologise for the noise.

NOTICE

The Tourist (4)......................... Office has moved to 245 Central Avenue.

WARNING

If you experience feelings like (5) .... or loss of appetite, stop taking the tablets immediately.

NOTICE

Mobile phones ruin other people's (6).................... of the film. Please switch yours off NOW!

Dress For Success

*Make a really good (7)...................
at that important job interview.
Wear a Longford suit!*

COMING SOON...

All the fun and (8)...............
of the circus on your computer
screen. **CyberCircus** the computer
game for the whole family!

School Rules

You are expected to do all the homework your teachers ask you to do. (9)............. is no excuse!

YOGA

*Get fit, learn to relax and improve your
(10) .... Come along to the
yoga classes at Fighting Fit Gym.
Every Thursday at 6 p.m.
from 5th March*

3 Put the nouns from exercises 1 and 2 into this table.

-ment	-ion/-ation
announcement	....
....	....
....	....
....	....
-ness	-ity
....	....
....	....

Reading

1 Read the article on the next page once quickly. Match the pictures to the paragraphs. There is an extra picture that you don't need to use.

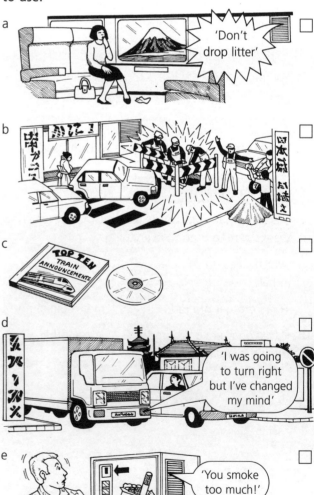

The Land of the talking machines

1 Japan is one of the noisiest countries in the world. Of course there are the usual city sounds but what makes Japan especially noisy are the thousands of recorded public announcements that the Japanese hear every day.

2 The moment you arrive at Narita International Airport in Tokyo you notice it. The escalator gently reminds you to hold on to your luggage. At the bank the cash machines actually ask you how much money you want. Even Japanese trucks tell you they are turning left or right as well as using their indicators.

3 In Japanese cities there are hundreds of different kinds of announcements. When you are walking along the street, they tell you to be careful. When you are waiting to get on the train, they tell you to stand behind the yellow line. When you are getting ready to get off the train, they tell you not to forget any of your belongings and while you are on the train they tell you not to drop litter or talk on your mobile phone because it disturbs other people. Even at the beach they warn you that the sand is hot!

4 A few people dislike the announcements enough to complain about them. A Tokyo university professor, Yoshimichi Nakajima, has written a book about the problem and it has become a bestseller. But for some Japanese the announcements are like music to their ears. The pop group SuperBell'Z, have made a CD with the ones you hear on trains. It's a big hit!

---

2 Some of the statements below are incorrect. Read the article again and find and correct the mistakes.

1 Japan is noisier than other countries because there are more of the usual city sounds.

2 When you arrive at the airport the escalators talk to you.

3 Of course you don't hear any announcements when you're walking along the street.

4 You are supposed to stand behind a yellow line while you wait for a train.

5 At the beach they tell you to take your shoes off.

6 Everyone really hates the announcements.

---

3 Find these words in the text, decide if they are verbs or nouns and choose the correct definition below. Circle your answer.

1 *notice* (paragraph 2)

  A a piece of writing that you put on a wall to give information to people

  B to feel, hear or see someone or something

2 *escalator* (paragraph 2)

  A moving stairs that carry people from one level of a building to another

  B getting bigger all the time

3 *reminds* (paragraph 2)

  A to make someone remember something that they must do

  B old clothes

4 *indicators* (paragraph 2)

  A shows

  B one of the lights on a vehicle which show which way it is going to turn

5 *belongings* (paragraph 3)

  A being someone's property

  B the things that you own or take with you somewhere

6 *litter* (paragraph 3)

  A waste paper, cans etc. that people leave on the ground

  B a group of young cats or dogs

7 *warn* (paragraph 3)

  A quite hot

  B to tell someone about a danger so that they can be careful and prepare for it

8 *bestseller* (paragraph 4)

  A a person who sells things

  B a book that a lot of people have bought

9 *hit* (paragraph 4)

  A to touch someone or something with a lot of force

  B a film, song, play etc. that is very successful

Speaking

1 📼 Look at these photographs and listen to someone describing them. Which photograph does she describe first?

1

2

2 📼 Listen again and complete these sentences.

1 I think it was taken in Switzerland because some of the people ....

2 It doesn't .... a very expensive restaurant.

3 The people ....
.... they're very good friends.

4 They ....
.... they know each other.

5 The man behind the counter ....

3 Complete the second sentence so that it is similar in meaning to the first sentence. Start and finish with the words in bold.

0 It looks cheap and friendly.
   It *looks like a cheap and friendly* ....
   place to eat.

1 She looks very tired.
   She ....
   she hasn't slept much.

2 He looks as if he's a busy person.
   He ....
   busy.

3 It looks expensive.
   It ....
   an expensive hotel.

4 It looks noisy.
   It ....
   people are making a lot of noise.

5 They look as if they are in their teens.
   They ....
   teenagers.

Writing: Paragraphs ▶ *Writing Reference page 149*

1 Here is a writing task and the letter a student wrote. The student didn't divide the letter into paragraphs. Mark the places where each paragraph ends.

Last week you went to see a film that you enjoyed very much.

Now you are writing a letter to an English-speaking friend to tell him/her about the film.

Say who was in the film, what it was about and why you enjoyed it so much.

Write about 100 words.

Dear Marek,

Thanks so much for your letter. I'm sorry it's taken me such a long time to answer but we've had exams and I've been really busy. I wanted to write and tell you about a (1) .... film I saw called Amelie. The (2) .... of the film is a young French actor called Audrey Tautou. She (3) .... a waitress who discovers an old box of toys in her apartment. She secretly returns it to its owner and his life changes completely. Because she can see that she has helped him so much, Amelie tries to help other people too, but she doesn't ever tell them. Then she meets a strange boy called Nino and falls in love. I won't tell you what happens in case you want to see it too. I thought it was one of the best films I've seen for a long time. I loved the (4) .... and I also think Audrey Tautou is a very good (5) .... There are great (6) .... of Paris too. Are there any good Polish films you'd suggest seeing?

All the best,

Anne

2 Choose the correct word for each space in the letter. Circle your answer.

1 A fantastic   B terrible   C boring
2 A person   B star   C character
3 A plays   B is   C acts
4 A story   B argument   C action
5 A director   B actor   C producer
6 A scenes   B films   C photographs

3 Find words for types of films in this wordsearch grid and match them to the film titles.

T	H	R	I	L	L	E	R
C	O	M	E	D	Y	E	O
T	R	S	S	A	D	V	M
H	R	T	C	Y	S	N	A
G	O	L	I	M	Y	T	N
H	R	Y	F	E	R	U	C
M	U	S	I	C	A	L	E

a) Independence Day

....

b) Romeo and Juliet

....

c) American Pie

....

d) The Fugitive

....

e) Scream

....

f) Chicago

....

Practice makes perfect?

Grammar 1: Past simple and past continuous ▶
CB page 31

About the language

Past simple

Form
Verb + *-ed* (remember there are many irregular verb forms)

Use
We use the **past simple**:
- to talk about events in the past which are now finished.
  *He **married** a woman who lived in the same village.*

- to talk about situations in the past.
  *They **lived** a normal life until he won the lottery.*

Past continuous

Form
was/were + -ing

Use
We use the **past continuous**:
- to talk about actions in progress in the past.
  *We **were** all **thinking** about our holidays.*

- to talk about an event that was in progress when another event happened. We often use **when** to link these two events.
  *They **were talking** about her **when** she **walked** into the room.*

- to talk about actions in progress at the same time in the past. We often use **while** to link these actions.
  ***While** Max **was cleaning** the living room, Sam **was washing** the dishes.*

! Typical mistakes ....

> *taught*
> She ~~teached~~ us how to use the internet.
> *didn't hear*
> I ~~was not hearing~~ what you said.
> *was studying*   *phoned*
> I ~~studied~~ for an exam when Alex ~~was phoning~~ to ask me out.

1 Use the prompts to write past simple sentences. All the verbs have irregular past forms.

0 Where / your father / live / when / he / be / a child?
Where did your father live when he was a child?

1 Who / win / the Eurovision Song Contest / last year?
....
....

2 What / you / do / last weekend?
....
....

3 He / not understand French very well / the first time he / go / to Paris.
....
....

4 We all / feel ill / after the meal.
....

5 Mike / throw / the car keys / and Tina / catch / them.
....
....

6 We / buy / Elena some perfume / for her birthday.
....
....

2   Choose the best alternative to complete these sentences.

0   The baby was finally falling asleep
   A   when the neighbours woke her up.   ☑
   B   while the neighbours were waking her up.   ☐

1   I didn't hear the phone because
   A   I was having a shower.   ☐
   B   I had a shower.   ☐

2   Sally was preparing the dinner
   A   while Bill was working on the computer.   ☐
   B   when Bill worked on the computer.   ☐

3   It was raining
   A   while we were getting to the beach.   ☐
   B   when we got to the beach.   ☐

4   I was going to visit my friend in hospital
   A   while I was seeing her drive past in a car.   ☐
   B   when I saw her drive past in a car.   ☐

3   Underline the correct tense, past simple or past continuous.

0   We *had/were having* breakfast when Tania *telephoned/was telephoning*.

1   I *saw/was seeing* my friend when I *got/was getting* to college.

2   Tina *fixed/was fixing* her motorcycle while Valentino *made/was making* lunch. Suddenly, they both *heard/were hearing* an explosion.

3   He *talked/was talking* on a mobile phone when a girl *came/was coming* up to him and *asked/was asking* for his autograph.

4   She *danced/was dancing* with another boy when her boyfriend *was walking/walked* into the discotheque.

5   I *tried/was trying* to talk to Simon while some workmen *dug/were digging* up the road outside. I couldn't even hear my own voice.

4   Complete this story using the past simple or the past continuous form of the verbs in brackets.

When Sandra and Oscar first (0) ....*met*.... (meet), she (1) .... (study) and he (2) .... (work) in a bank. He (3) .... (like) her immediately and he (4) .... (decide) to ask her out to dinner. He (5) .... (choose) a small Italian restaurant near the hospital. When he (6) .... (arrive) to pick her up, she (7) .... (wait) at the entrance. She (8) .... (wear) a blue shirt and a pair of jeans. He (9) .... (think) she looked wonderful. At the restaurant the waiter (10) .... (take) them to their table. They (11) .... (enjoy) a fantastic meal, but while they (12) .... (wait) for the bill, Oscar (13) .... (realise) he had left his wallet at home. He (14) .... (not know) what to do. He was just about to tell her that he (15) .... (not have) any money when she (16) .... (say) 'Why don't you let me pay? My parents have just sent me some money.' He (17) .... (feel) a little bit embarrassed but he really (18) .... (not have) any choice. He (19) .... (explain) the situation and she said she (20) .... (not mind) at all.

Grammar 2: Past perfect simple ▶
CB page 35

About the language

Past perfect simple

Form
had + past participle

Use
We use the **past perfect simple**:
• to talk about a time earlier than another past time. We often use adverbs like **when**, or **by the time** before the later time and **already** with the earlier time.

   By the time I **got** to the market, most of the stalls **had already closed.**

⟩ **Typical mistakes** • • • • • • • • • •

   seen
As soon as the film started, I realised I had ~~seed~~ it before.

   had
By the time I ~~had~~ got to the station my train ⱡ left.

1   <u>Underline</u> the best alternative.

SPORTS TODAY
8th JULY 2003

Reginaldo hurts knee!

SPORTS TODAY
14th JULY 2003

Brazil wins cup without Reginaldo!

0   Reginaldo *didn't play*/hadn't played in the match because he hurt/*had hurt* his knee.

1   Cristina didn't talk/hadn't talked to Peter at the party because he was/had been very rude to her the day before.

2   Karina didn't understand/hadn't understood why she failed/had failed the exam.

3   They didn't watch/hadn't watched their favourite programme last night because their TV stopped/had stopped working in the morning.

4   Simon had grown/grew a beard during the summer so none of us recognised/had recognised him.

5   Oscar left/had left his wallet at home so Sandra paid/had paid for the meal.

6   When I saw/had seen Jennifer at the party, she just returned/had just returned from Paris.

7   When we parked/had parked our car we walked/had walked to the town centre.

8   I felt/had felt nervous at first on my new motorbike because I didn't ride/hadn't ridden a motorbike for many years.

2   Complete these sentences, using either the past simple or the past perfect form of the verbs in brackets.

1   No one .... why Sonia .... to class that day. (know, not come)

2   Last week I .... someone who .... never .... on a plane. (meet, be)

3   Susanna .... me last night. I .... from her for weeks. (phone, not hear)

4   We .... three videos and then we .... we .... them all before. (borrow, realise, see)

5   When I .... to the restaurant, my friends .... already .... a table. (get, find).

6   Nina and Olivier .... the last week of their holiday in Paris. They .... already .... Spain and Portugal. (spend, visit)

3   Correct the mistakes students made with the past simple, past continuous and past perfect.

1

One day last week my friend Sophie and I decided to see what was on TV. She had the remote control and kept changing the channel. I had been so bored I decided to read a book. I was so interested in the book that by the time I had realised how late it was, my favourite programme already finished.

2

We had waited for a bus for about twenty minutes but it didn't come. In the end, we had got a taxi, but by the time we had got to the station the train already went.

3

We went to the supermarket to get some things for lunch but when we had got to the checkout André had realised he didn't have his wallet. He remembered that while we waited for the train he was feeling someone push past him. We had realised this person took the wallet.

Vocabulary 1: Education ▶ *CB page 33*

1   Choose the best alternative to complete these sentences.

1 I didn't go to nursery ....
   A college   B school   C garden

2 There are very good .... schools near here.
   A First and Second   B Child and Teenager
   C Primary and Secondary

3 When can you .... school in your country?
   A stop   B leave   C end

4 I decided to .... the exam again in September.
   A make   B present   C take

5 I want to do a .... course in engineering.
   A degree   B superior   C career

6 It is always fun to see your friends at the beginning of a new academic ....
   A course   B term   C year

7 What .... are you studying this year?
   A subjects   B courses   C matters

8 Both my brothers are studying .... universities in Britain.
   A in   B at   C to

2   Complete the dictionary definitions of university courses (1–11) with words from the wordsearch grid.

S	E	L	A	W	B	I	C	E	P
H	T	P	R	Y	I	H	O	N	H
P	S	Y	C	H	O	L	O	G	Y
H	C	I	H	I	L	E	M	I	S
I	O	B	I	S	O	C	E	N	I
L	W	A	T	T	G	O	D	E	C
O	E	C	E	O	Y	N	I	E	S
S	O	N	C	R	M	O	C	R	E
O	H	I	T	Y	D	M	I	I	C
P	S	T	U	N	E	I	N	N	A
H	P	H	R	C	H	C	E	G	R
Y	C	H	E	M	I	S	T	R	Y

1 .... (n) the science of studying chemicals and what happens to them when they change or combine with each other

2 .... (n) the work of designing roads, bridges, machines etc.

3 .... (n) the scientific study of living things

4 .... (n) the treatment and study of illness and injuries

5 .... (n) the study of legal rules and regulations

6 .... (n) the study of the mind

7 .... (n) the study of the way a country produces money and things to sell

8 .... (n) the study of the things that happened in the past

9 .... (n) the study of designing buildings

10 .... (n) the study of ideas about life and how people should live

11 .... (n) the study of things that happen naturally in the world such as heat, light or movement

3   Now complete these sentences about yourself.

1 The subjects I enjoy most are ....
   ....

2 I'd like to study ....
   at university.

3 I will have to study for ....
   years.

Vocabulary 2: Adverbs of manner ▶
CB page 36

About the language

Adverbs of manner

Use

- **Adverbs of manner** tell us about verbs. They tell us how somebody does something or how something happens. They usually come after the verb in the sentence.
  *She writes very **neatly**.*

- We use **adjectives** to tell us about **nouns**. They can come before the noun in a sentence.
  *She has very **neat** writing.*

Form

- Most adverbs of manner are formed with the adjective plus *-ly*.
  nervous – nervously
  beautiful – beautifully

- Adverbs from adjectives that end in *-y* end *-ily*.
  angry – angrily

- Some adverbs are irregular.
  good – well

- Some adverbs have the same form as the adjective.
  hard – hard
  fast – fast

Typical mistakes

He writes very confident̷. ^ly

She works very hard̷l̷y̷.

A: How was the exam?
B: Quite ~~well~~. ^good

She did ~~good~~ in the exam. ^well

He doesn't drive very careful̷l̷y̷.

The children were playing happ̷y̷ly. ^i

1   Underline the correct alternative to complete these sentences.

0   Carmen speaks English and Italian very *confident/<u>confidently</u>*.

1   She sings *beautiful/beautifully* and plays the piano *good/well*.

2   She is also a *successful/successfully* writer of children's books.

3   Nevertheless, she's not a very *good/well* cook.

4   She also sews *bad/badly* and has no idea how to knit.

5   She lives *happy/happily* with her husband and twin sons.

6   The only problem is that they live in a very *noisy/noisily* part of the city.

7   They are so tired of the noise that they are thinking *serious/seriously* of moving to the countryside.

2   Write the adverb forms of these adjectives.

1   noisy   ....

2   successful   ....

3   happy   ....

4   careful   ....

5   clear   ....

6   easy   ....

3   Complete this text using the words from the box.

| fast   hard   well |

I really wanted to do (1) .... in the test. I am a (2) .... worker, so I didn't start revising until a couple of days before. I studied quite (3) .... for two or three days and thought I would remember everything quite (4) .... When I saw the test questions though, I got a nasty shock. They were really (5) .... – much more difficult than I had thought they would be. To make matters worse, the test was really long. There were more than 100 questions! I wrote very (6) .... but I still couldn't finish it in time.

Listening

1 You will hear Jonathan Davie, a young actor, talking about an audition for an acting school. Before you listen, look at the pictures and try to put them in order.

a

b

c

d

e

f

2 Listen to the recording and decide if the order is correct.

3 For each question, tick (✓) the best answer.

1 How did Jonathan find out about the famous acting school?
  A He saw an advertisement in the newspaper. ☐
  B He saw a website about acting schools. ☐
  C A girl told him about it. ☐

2 Why hadn't Jonathan learnt a speech?
  A He already knew a lot of speeches. ☐
  B He didn't know that it was necessary. ☐
  C He decided not to learn one. ☐

3 Why was the girl upset at the end of her audition?
  A She had forgotten her speech. ☐
  B They told her that she hadn't done it very well. ☐
  C They stopped her before she had finished her speech. ☐

4 Why did Jonathan feel stupid?
  A Because he was so nervous. ☐
  B Because other people had used the same speech. ☐
  C Because he forgot the speech. ☐

5 What happened at the end of his audition?
  A They told him he had failed the audition. ☐
  B They told him that he had done very well. ☐
  C They told him to learn a different speech. ☐

6 How did Jonathan prepare for the second audition?
  A He chose another speech and practised it a lot. ☐
  B He practised the same speech. ☐
  C He practised with the girl who had played Juliet. ☐

4 Listen again to check your answers.

Writing: Story ▶ *Writing Reference page 155*

⚡ **Time expressions**

• We use these time expressions to show when events and actions happen in a story:

one afternoon (morning, night etc.)
One afternoon last summer a friend invited me to go sailing with her.

at first
At first I didn't want to go because I'm a bit scared of boats.

after a while
The sea was very calm when we set out but after a while it began to get much rougher.

finally
My friend had trouble controlling the sails and I couldn't really help her. Finally we got back to the shore.

• Look at these definitions.
at first in the beginning
firstly adverb used before saying the first of several things.

Which expression should you use in these sentences?
A: *Why isn't Alessandro in the team?*
B: *At first/Firstly because he hasn't been to the training sessions, secondly because he isn't very fast and thirdly because he gets on badly with Reginaldo.*

At first/Firstly she seemed quite friendly but later I realised she didn't like me very much.

1 Read this story. Then choose the correct word for each space. Circle your answer.

Practice makes perfect

I went skiing for the first time last winter. (1) ...., a boy asked if I would like to ski down from the top of the mountain with him.

(2) .... I thought this was a wonderful idea but when we got to the top, I wasn't so sure. The boy said that it would be all right and we started to ski down very slowly.

(3) .... I began to feel more confident about my skiing. Then, suddenly, I hit a bump and fell over. I hadn't hurt myself but I felt very embarrassed. The boy helped me up and we continued skiing.

(4) .... we got to the bottom of the mountain. I was tired but very pleased that I had done it.

---

1 A One morning   B At first

2 A Firstly   B At first

3 A After a while   B One day

4 A Secondly   B Finally

2 Write a story in your notebook using these pictures and the word prompts below.

a

b

c

d

e

f

a) I / watch / some young people / play / beach volleyball

b) girl / invite / me / join the game

c) I / start / play / serve / ball / into / net

d) girl / show / how / serve / properly

e) I / try / again / this time / a great serve / everyone / cheer

f) end of the game / everyone / congratulate / me / feel / very /happy

Behind the mask

Grammar 1: Reported statements ▶ *CB page 39*

About the language

Reported speech

- We use **reported speech** to tell people what someone said or wrote. The **tenses** usually change in **reported speech**. They move one step back into the past.

Direct Speech		Reported Speech
I **don't like** wearing make-up.	⇨	Tania said she **didn't like** wearing make-up.
I **didn't see** the exhibition.	⇨	Marek told me he **hadn't seen** the exhibition.
I **will write** to Tom.	⇨	Luisa said she **would** write to Tom.
I **can't come** before 10.30.	⇨	Mike told us he **couldn't** come before 10.30.

- **Time phrases** also change in reported speech

I saw a good film **last night**.	⇨	He said he had seen a good film **the night before./the previous night**.
I'll be in Paris **next month**.	⇨	She said she would be in Paris **the following month**.

- The two most common **reporting verbs** are *tell* and *say*. When we use *tell* we use an object. When we use *say* we do not use an object.

  He **told us** he would probably be late.
  He **said** he had to go to the bank before the meeting.

1 Complete the examples in this table.

Direct speech ⇨ Reported speech
Present simple ⇨ Past simple
'I sometimes wear lipstick.'   She said she (0) *sometimes wore lipstick.*   'I have a shower every morning.'   He said he (1) ....
Past simple ⇨ Past perfect
'I enjoyed the exhibition.'   He told us he (2) ....
will ⇨ would
'I'll post the letter.'   She said she (3) ....
can ⇨ could
'I can speak Spanish.'   She told us she (4) ....
Time phrases
last night ⇨ (5) .....*the night before*.........   next week ⇨ (6) ....   yesterday ⇨ (7) ....   last month ⇨ (8) ....   next year ⇨ (9) ....

> **Typical mistakes** · · · · · · · · · · · · · · ·
>
>   *would*
> She said she ~~will~~ be here on Tuesday.
>
>   *told*
> Lucy ~~said~~ us that she wanted to stay for three weeks.
>
>   *said*
> Luke ~~told~~ he hadn't ever been to Spain.

2   Put these sentences into reported speech.

0   I saw a great exhibition yesterday.

He said he had seen a great exhibition the day before.   .

1   I bought a new jacket last week.

She told me ....

....

2   I'll be in London next week.

He said ....

....

3   I want to do a postgraduate course next year.

She said ....

....

4   I can come next Wednesday.

She told me ....

....

5   I didn't watch television last night.

He said ....

....

6   I can't play the piano.

He told me ....

....

3   Put a tick (✓) next to the correct sentences. Correct the other sentences.

0   She ~~said~~ *told* me that she didn't wear make-up.

00   He told us that he could speak Russian. ✓

1   She told she would be at home on Saturday night.

2   My teacher said I had to study harder.

3   I told them that I didn't want to play.

4   Carla said us she had tried to phone.

5   He told I could borrow his bike.

Grammar 2: Reported questions ▶ *CB page 43*

About the language

Reported questions

In **reported questions** the verb tenses and all the other words change in the same way as in **reported statements**. There are two types of **reported question**.

- In **reported *wh*-questions** the word order is:
  Question word + subject + verb

Direct question	Reported question
Where is Simon living?	⇨ *She asked me where Simon was living.*
Where does he work?	⇨ *She asked me where he worked.*

- In **reported *Yes/No* questions** we use *if* or *whether*. The word order is:
  if/whether + subject + verb

Direct question	Reported question
Does he live in Hollywood?	⇨ *She asked me if he lived in Hollywood.*
Is he married?	⇨ *She asked me whether he was married.*
Have you seen his latest film?	⇨ *She asked me if I had seen his latest film.*

1   Complete the second sentence so that it is similar in meaning to the first sentence. Start with the words given.

0   'Who is your favourite actor?' she asked.

She asked me *who my favourite actor was*.

1   'Why do you like him?' she asked.

She asked me ....

2   'When did he start acting?' she asked.

She asked me ....

3   'Which films has he acted in?' she asked.

She asked me ....

4   'When did you see his last film?' she asked.

She asked me ....

5   'Where does he live?' she asked.

She asked me ....

6   'Who is he married to?' she asked.

She asked me ....

2 Put these questions into reported speech.

0 Do you find Brad Pitt attractive?

He asked me if I found Brad Pitt
.
attractive.

1 Do you think he is more attractive than Ben Affleck?

....

2 Do you think he is a good actor?

....

3 Did you enjoy his latest film?

....

4 Was Jennifer Aniston in it too?

....

5 Have you seen the TV series *Friends*?

....

6 Have you seen any films starring Courtney Cox?

....

7 Are you going to the cinema this weekend?

....

8 Can I come with you?

....

Vocabulary 1: Phrasal verbs with *get* ▶
CB page 40

About the language

Phrasal verbs with *get*

A **phrasal verb** is a verb and a particle (like *on*, *through* or *over*) which has a different meaning to the verb on its own.

I don't get on with my older brother very well. (I don't have a friendly relationship with my older brother.)

1 Match the first half of the sentence in Column A with the second half of the sentence in Column B.

A

0 I tried to find out what time the film started …
1 She got away with being rude …
2 Prices have gone up so much …
3 I always cycle to work in the morning …
4 I've always got on well with …
5 It took her a couple of weeks …

B

a) to get over the flu.
b) but I couldn't get through to the cinema.
c) because the teacher didn't hear what she said.
d) to get round the traffic congestion problem in our town.
e) my cousins.
f) I find it difficult to get by.

0 *b*   1 ......   2 ......   3 ......   4 ......   5 ......

2 Put the phrases from the box into the table.

her neighbours   a difficulty   the manager
not handing in your homework   breaking up with Carlos

Phrasal verb collocations	
get on with	my brother, *her neighbours* ....
get over	the flu, ...
get through to	the cinema box office, ...
get round	a problem, ...
get away with	being rude, ...

3 Complete these sentences using the collocations in the tables on page 35.

1 My friend Sonia is going to look for a new flat because she doesn't get ....

2 Flavio always gets .... because the teacher likes him so much.

3 I tried to get .... of the company but no one answered the phone.

4 One of the biggest .... I had to get .... was not speaking the language.

5 Sometimes I think my friend Eva will never get .... She still talks about him all the time.

Vocabulary 2: Learning phrasal verbs

Here is a suggestion a student made about how to learn phrasal verbs. Look at these pictures the student drew and match them to the phrasal verbs you used in exercises 2 and 3.

I think about the meaning of the phrasal verb and draw a picture to help me remember it.

1 ....

2 ....

3 ....

4 ....

5 ....

Vocabulary 3: Physical appearance ▶
CB page 44

About the language
Physical appearance

Beauty:	attractive, beautiful, good-looking, plain
Height:	short, medium height, tall
Weight/build:	overweight, well-built, slim, thin, skinny
Hair (face):	beard, moustache
Hair (head):	curly, wavy, straight, blonde

1 🔊 Listen to a student. Tick (✓) the two photographs she describes.

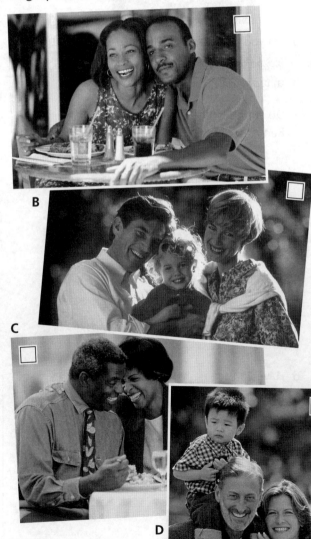

A

B

C

D

2   Complete these sentences from the student's description.

1   The woman has dark .... hair and the man is .... with a ....

2   The woman is .... and .... but the man is quite ....

3   She looks like their daughter because she is .... and so are the man and woman.

4   The little girl has got .... hair but the woman has .... hair.

3   Complete these descriptions using the language in the box.

> ~~beautiful~~   overweight   beard   slim
> medium height   attractive

A

One of my favourite people is my aunt Stefanie. She is in her fifties now but I've seen photos of her when she was younger and she was very (0) *beautiful*. In my opinion, she still is. She isn't tall and she isn't short. I suppose you would say that she is (1) .... She does a lot of exercise so she is always quite (2) .... even though she never goes on diets.

B

My brother-in-law, Tony is one of the people in my family I am closest to. He and my sister both love food so they are always a bit (3) .... It doesn't matter though because they are both very (4) ...., in my opinion. They've both got dark hair and eyes and Tony has got a (5) .... at the moment. He usually shaves it off in the summer though.

Speaking

1   Look at these conversations and mark them AC (agreeing completely), AP (agreeing partly) D (disagreeing) and DS (disagreeing strongly).

1

A: *I think* people use their cars too much. We should all try to use public transport or ride bicycles.

B: *I agree up to a point*, *but* some people need to use their cars for their work.

....

2

A: *In my opinion*, teachers give children too much homework. They don't have any time to play.

B: *Oh, I don't really agree. I think* it's important for children to understand that life isn't just playing.

....

3

A: *I think* teenagers shouldn't be allowed out after 11 p.m.

B: *I don't agree at all!* Where I live most of the clubs and discotheques don't even open before 1 a.m.

....

4

A: *In my opinion*, footballers earn too much money. They are often very young and irresponsible.

B: *That's right!* They don't know how to spend their money and they often don't play very well either.

....

5

A: *I think* eating in fast food restaurants is bad for your health. The food is usually really terrible.

B: *Oh, I don't really agree.* Some fast food restaurants serve very healthy things like salads.

....

2   Complete this conversation with different expressions from exercise 1 for expressing opinions, agreeing and disagreeing.

Sara: (0) *I think* people spend too much money on their appearance.

Maria: (1) ....
            but looking attractive is important.

Paulo: (2) ....
            Attractive people earn more money.

Claudia: (3) ....
            that's really unfair.

Sara: (4) ....
            it shouldn't matter what someone looks like.

Maria: (5) ....
            It's important in some jobs.

Claudia: Well, it shouldn't be.

Paulo: (6) ....
            Models and actors have to be attractive.

3   🖥 Now listen and compare your answers.

4   Complete this conversation using the prompts in brackets.

Donatella: (1) (*express opinion*) ....
            smoking should be banned in public places.

Carla: (2) (*disagree completely*) ....
            .... People like to smoke when they go out at night.

Marek: (3) (*agree completely*) ....
            .... If you smoke outside it doesn't affect anyone else.

Bea: (4) (*disagree*) ....
            If you're standing next to someone, you can still smell the smoke.

Donatella: (5) (*agree completely*) ....
            Doctors say that breathing in other people's smoke causes cancer.

Carla: (6) (*express opinion*) ....
            people should be allowed to choose.

Bea: (7) (*agree partly*) ....
            but only if their choices don't affect other people.

Writing: Story ▶ *Writing Reference page 150*

⚡ Conjunctions
We can join two sentences by using **conjunctions**. We do not need to use a comma.
They moved to a new house. They got on very well with their neighbours.
*They moved to a new house **and** they got on very well with their neighbours.*

Here are some conjunctions.

Conjunction	Use	Example
and	giving extra information	*They moved to a new house **and** they got on very well with their neighbours.*
but	giving different information	*They moved to a new house **but** they didn't get on with their new neighbours.*
because	giving a reason	*They moved to a new house **because** they didn't get on with their old neighbours.*
so	giving a consequence	*They didn't get on with their neighbours **so** they moved to a new house.*
although	to show that something is surprising	*They moved to a new house **although** they got on very well with their old neighbours.*

1   Choose a linking word from the table above to join these pairs of sentences.

0 Olivia and Carlos got married. They went to live in France.

Olivia and Carlos got married and they went to live in France.

1   Carlos couldn't find a job. He stayed at home and looked after the house.

....

2   Olivia wanted to stay at home with Carlos. They needed money.

....

3   She had to find a job. She started looking at the job advertisements in the newspaper.

....

4   She started working in an English school. The salary wasn't very good.

....

5   It was quite expensive living in France. They could only just get by.

....

6   Olivia made lots of friends. Her French wasn't very good.

....

7   She could understand it quite well. She couldn't speak very much.

....

8   Carlos spoke French fluently. He had studied it at university.

....

9   He didn't have many opportunities to speak it. He was at home all day.

....

10   He started to feel lonely. He joined the local drama club.

....

2   Rewrite these sentences and make them more interesting by using the words in the box.

>   heartbroken   ~~delighted~~   terrified
>   disgusting   sternly   furious   handsome

0   He was very pleased with his new clothes.

   He was delighted with his new clothes.

....

1   There was a bad smell coming from the kitchen.

....

2   She told him seriously that he would have to leave.

....

3   Where the frog had been before there was an attractive prince.

....

4   She was afraid when she saw the Big Friendly Giant.

....

5   When she saw her boyfriend in the street with another girl, she was angry.

....

6   She was very sad when she saw the Beast lying in the garden.

....

3   Look at this task and the story a student wrote. Rewrite it in your notebook, using conjunctions and the adjectives from exercise 2 to make it more interesting.

> You are going to write a story. Your story must begin with the words 'I had never believed in ghosts until that night in March.' It should be about 100 words.

I had never believed in ghosts until that night in March. I was staying in an old castle. I woke up in the middle of the night. There was a bad smell in my room. I looked around to try and find where it was coming from. I saw a figure carrying its head under its arm. I was afraid. I spoke to it very seriously. I told it to go away. It put its head on its shoulders. It turned around. It smiled at me. I realised it was a rather attractive ghost. It disappeared.

Next morning the man who owned the house was pleased when I told the story. He said it was the ghost of his great-great-great-grandfather. No one had seen him for 100 years!

UNIT

6 Whatever next?

Grammar 1: *will* and *going to* ▶ *CB page 49*

About the language

will and *going to*

- We use *will* + infinitive to talk about **decisions made at the moment of speaking (sudden decisions)**. We cannot use *going to* + infinitive in this case.

  *I think **I'll** have an apple. I'm really hungry.*

- We use *going to* + infinitive to talk about **decisions made before the moment of speaking (plans and intentions)**. We cannot use *will* + infinitive in this case.

  A: *Are you **going to visit** your friends in France again this summer?*

  B: *No, I'm **going to do** a computer course. I've already paid for it.*

- We use *will* + infinitive for **predicting something that we know or believe something about**.

  *I think Valencia **will beat** Real Madrid. They're a much better team.*

- We use *going to* + infinitive for **predicting something that we can see, feel or hear some evidence about now**. We cannot use present continuous in this case.

  *Look at those clouds. It's **going to rain**.*

> **Typical mistakes** ·············
>
>   *ll meet*
> *We're going to meet you outside the cinema at 6.15. OK?*
>
>   *is going to study*
> *She ~~will study~~ architecture at university next year.*
>
>   *'m going to sneeze*
> *Give me a tissue. I ~~will sneeze.~~*

1 Use *will* and the verbs in the box to write what these people are saying or thinking.

order	finish	have	~~go~~	wear

0

I think _____ *I'll go* _____ to bed.

1

I think _____ my jeans with the red shirt.

2

_____ it tomorrow.

3

_____ a take-away pizza instead!

4

I think _____ a coke. What about you?

2 Complete these sentences, using *going to* and the verbs in the box.

play   cook   get   ~~buy~~   deliver

0 I don't know what to get Dad for Christmas but I*'m going to buy* Mum some perfume. I've already decided.

1 Susan doesn't eat meat so I .... a vegetarian dish specially for her. I've already bought the vegetables.

2 We couldn't book the tennis court for Saturday so we .... on Sunday instead.

3 Gloria's parents are really amazing. They .... her a big screen TV if she passes her exams.

4 I've paid for my new sofa and the people from the shop .... it tomorrow morning.

3 Complete these sentences with *going to* or *will*.

0 It*'s going to be* hot tomorrow. Look at the sky.

1 Gema .... get top marks in the test. She always does!

2 Prices .... go up again. At least that's what the papers say.

3 Apparently, some of the companies that make robots .... try to make one that really looks like a human being.

4 Digital cameras .... get cheaper soon. They've been available for a couple of years now.

5 I think I .... be sick. I feel really terrible.

4 Complete this conversation with *going to* or *will*.

Bettina: You (0) ....*will*....... be pleased to hear that I (1) .... get a mobile phone after all.

Alberto: At last! I'm sure you (2) .... find it really useful. I (3) .... be able to get in touch with you wherever you are! Have you decided what kind you (4) .... get?

Bettina: Well, I can't make up my mind. I think I (5) .... get either a Nokia or a Motorola.

Alberto: When (6) .... buy it?

Bettina: I'm not sure. I (7) .... let you know and you can come with me. By the way, I've bought a tennis racquet and I've decided I (8) .... start playing.

Alberto: (9) .... have lessons?

Bettina: No, (10) .... teach me!

Grammar 2: Present simple and present continuous for future ▶ *CB page 52*

About the language

Present continuous for future

We use the present continuous to talk about **plans and arrangements** (things that have already been decided). We cannot use *will* + infinitive in this case.

I'm seeing the dentist tomorrow at 5 p.m.

Present simple for future

We use the present simple to talk about **timetables and programmes**.

Next term starts on 3rd October.

> **Typical mistakes**
>
> *'m going to go out*
> *I ~~will go out~~ with Eva on Friday night.*
>
> *leaves*
> *The train ~~is going to leave~~ at 6.30.*

1   Complete the sentences with the information in these texts.

> **Museum opening times:**
> Daily 10–6. Wednesdays closed.

0

1

> *July 17th 8.00 p.m.*
> *Dinner with Alicia.*

2

> **1st April**
> **London–Paris 9 a.m.**

3

> **Photography summer school**
> **15th — 31st August**

4

> *Pick Pablo up at Heathrow*
> *Airport 2.30 p.m.*

0 The museum ....*opens*............... at 10 p.m.

1 Charlotte .... dinner with Alicia at 8.00 p.m.

2 Our train .... for Paris at 9 a.m.

3 The course .... on 15th August and .... on 31st August.

4 Andrea .... Pablo from Heathrow Airport at 2.30 p.m..

2   Underline the correct verb form to complete this extract from a letter.

> I think I told you that I had entered a competition to win a holiday in Portugal. Well, I won and I (0) *will come/am coming* to Portugal next month! I collected my airline tickets yesterday.
>
> Unfortunately my flight (1) *leaves/is going to leave* at a really terrible time – 3 o'clock in the morning on August 2nd! The good thing about it is that it (2) *gets/is going to get* to Lisbon early in the morning.
>
> I (3) *will go/am going* on a tour of the north of Portugal which (4) *starts/is going to start* on Friday morning, the day after I (5) *arrive/will arrive*. (6) *Are you doing/Will you do* anything on the evening of Thursday 2nd? It's the only time I have free and I'd love to see you.

Vocabulary: Collocations ▶
CB page 51

1   Complete these sentences using a preposition from the box.

to	with	~~in~~	to	at	of
	on	of	from		

0 Learning to design websites interests me.

  I'm interested ....*in*........... learning to design websites.

1 I design things really well.

  I'm very good .... designing things.

2 I've always liked technology too.

  I've always been keen .... technology.

3 Technology frightens a lot of girls.

  A lot of girls are afraid .... technology.

4 I'm not really like any of my friends.

  I'm completely different .... my friends.

5 I don't know why they behave in the way they do.

  I don't know what's wrong .... them.

6 They don't seem to know about things like the Internet.

  They don't seem to be aware .... things like the Internet.

7 They're like girls from the last century.

  They're similar .... girls from the last century.

8 But if I criticise them they get really upset.

  They're very sensitive .... criticism.

2   Write questions for these answers using the words in brackets.

0   (sports/keen)

What sports are you most keen on?

Well, I like tennis and football and I also enjoy swimming.

1   (subjects/good)

....

....

I always do well in maths and science subjects.

2   (member of family/similar)

....

....

My brother, Daniel. We're identical twins!

3   (kinds of music/interested)

....

....

I'd really like to find out more about computer music but jazz interests me too.

4   (things/worried)

....

....

My exams!

5   (member of your family/most different)

....

....

Probably my sister. She hates sport and she doesn't like technological things either.

6   (things/most afraid)

....

....

Spiders! No, seriously ... wars are the things that frighten me most.

3   Read this conversation and choose the correct word for each space. Circle your answer.

Alberto: So how often do you (0) .... your email?

Bettina: At least once a day and sometimes more. If I've (1) .... any messages I usually answer them straightaway and I always (2) .... my friends messages on their birthdays.

Alberto: I use my computer mostly for (3) ....

Bettina: Don't you ever (4) .... the net?

Alberto: Sure, in fact I (5) .... a fantastic website just the other day. It was the official site of the film *A.I.* You can actually chat to a robot on the site!

Bettina: And do you ever buy things (6) ....?

Alberto: Well, I bought some CDs and a new ring tone for my mobile phone this morning.

Bettina: You really like your mobile, don't you? What's the worst experience you've ever had with a computer?

Alberto: Once, when I had to hand in a really important essay the next day, my computer (7) .... and I (8) .... the whole document.

Bettina: Hadn't you (9) .... a backup copy?

Alberto: No. Anyway it turns out the computer (10) .... a virus so the copy probably would have been infected too.

0	A	look	B	see	Ⓒ check	D	watch
1	A	received	B	arrived	C	retrieved	D	accessed
2	A	give	B	send	C	emit	D	put
3	A	word producing	B	word processing	C	word writing	D	word working
4	A	navigate	B	sail	C	travel	D	surf
5	A	arrived at	B	reached	C	travelled	D	visited
6	A	online	B	on hold	C	connected	D	plugged in
7	A	dropped	B	crashed	C	hung up	D	closed
8	A	missed	B	lost	C	disappeared	D	rubbed
9	A	done	B	made	C	produced	D	prepared
10	A	was with	B	took	C	had	D	suffered

Reading

1   You are going to read a magazine article about a robot exhibition. Scan the text to find where the robots in the photos are mentioned. Write the paragraph number in the box.

A Asimo

B Paro

C Posy
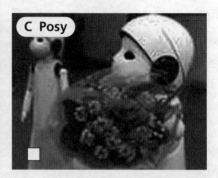

D T7S Type 2

E SDR-4X

Loveable robots

1   Most of the robots in the Robodex exhibition in Yokohama, Japan can talk, climb stairs or pick up objects but Posy, the little girl robot, doesn't do any of these things. She is designed to look loveable. Posy is one of a new generation of robots. Their designers don't want them to seem frightening to human beings.

2   There are still many technological problems to solve before people start buying robots to have in their homes, but scientists realise there is a psychological problem as well. Machines that look like humans make many of us feel anxious.

3   'The theme of Robodex is robots that co-exist with humans,' said Toshi Doi. Toshi is the designer of Aibo, the robot pet and SDR-4X, a singing, dancing machine and one of the most impressive robots at the show. Another is Honda's new robot called Asimo. The company hopes it will one day be able to do household tasks.

4   Japan is already home to half the world's industrial robots and 90% of robot pets. 'I don't think we feel uncomfortable with robots and we also love technology,' said Kazuo Hirai of Honda.

5   The robots that appeal most to humans at the moment, however, are those that don't have a human form. Paro, a furry creature a bit like a seal, is used in children's hospitals all over the world because the pleasant sensation of holding him helps the children recover more quickly.

6   Not all robots are designed to be appealing however. For example, there's the robot guard dog T7S Type 2. He has a camera and a mobile phone and can be guided by voice commands so that if you are away on holiday, you can phone him and tell him what to do.

2   Read the text again. For each question, choose the correct answer A, B, C or D.

1 Why is Posy different from other robots?
   A She can climb stairs.
   B She doesn't do anything.
   C She can talk.
   D She is feminine.

2 Why would someone read the text?
   A To find out more about robots.
   B To find out how to get to Robodex.
   C To learn about how robots are built.
   D To find out whether people like robots.

3 Why haven't robots become popular yet?
   A They don't look enough like real people.
   B They don't work properly.
   C People find them strange and frightening.
   D They are too ugly.

4 What is Paro?
   A A robot pet.
   B A robot nurse.
   C A robot child.
   D A robot doctor.

5 What is the writer trying to do in the text?
   A Persuade people to buy robots.
   B Explain how robots work.
   C Criticise robots.
   D Describe some robots.

3   Find adjectives in the text to fill in the gaps in these dictionary definitions.

1 If something is .... , it is nice and easy to love.

2 If something is .... , it makes you feel afraid.

3 If you feel .... , you feel very worried.

4 If something is .... , it is very good and you admire it.

5 If you feel .... , you feel embarrassed or worried.

6 If something is .... , it is nice and enjoyable.

7 If something is .... , it is attractive or interesting.

4   Use the adjectives from exercise 3 to complete these sentences.

1 I don't find the idea of going skiing very ....

2 I felt very .... when my friend gave me such an expensive present.

3 Their new home cinema centre is really ....

4 Fluffy is not a very intelligent cat but he certainly is ....

5 She had a very .... experience walking home alone one night.

6 Did you have a .... time with Jill and Dave?

7 He was so .... about his exams that he couldn't sleep.

Listening

1   🖭 You will hear a conversation between a girl and a boy about technology. Listen and put a tick (✓) by the things they mention.

1 mobile phones ☐
2 robots ☐
3 video cameras ☐
4 email ☐
5 the Internet ☐
6 CD players ☐
7 computer ☐

2   Before you listen again, look at these statements and decide if they are true (T) or false (F).

1 The experiment lasted a week. ☐

2 Bettina doesn't have a mobile phone. ☐

3 The man was allowed to use his computer. ☐

4 The man didn't mind about not using his mobile phone. ☐

5 He didn't like not being able to use his email. ☐

6 He got the information he needed from a library. ☐

7 After the experiment the man decided to stop using modern technology. ☐

3   🖭 Listen to the conversation again to see if you were right.

Writing: Notes and messages ▶ *Writing Reference page 151*

We write notes and messages when we want to say something very briefly to someone we know very well.

In notes and messages we often do the following:

- use abbreviations instead of the full form
- use imperatives and *Can you ...* instead of polite requests
- leave out words like articles, pronouns (*I*, *we* etc.) and auxiliary verbs
- leave out other unnecessary things like *I am writing to tell you ...; How are you?; your friend ...; this telephone number* etc.
- begin without writing *Dear ...*
- finish without writing *Love*, *All the best*, etc.

Dear Gloria,
     Gone
~~I have gone~~ to ~~the~~ *cinema with* ~~my friend~~
       Back   *p.m.*   *Can you*
Carmen. ~~I will be back~~ *this* ~~afternoon.~~ ~~Would you~~
   feed
~~mind feeding the~~ *cats?*
     See
~~I am looking forward to seeing~~ *you later.*

~~Love,~~

Cecilia

1 Use abbreviations from exercises 2 and 3 on page 53 of the Coursebook to complete this crossword.

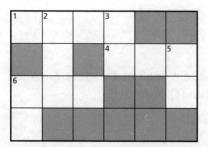

Clues across

1 as soon as possible
4 Monday
6 and so on

Clues down

2 Saturday
3 afternoon
5 Please note
6 for example

2 Cross out the words you don't need to use in these messages and change the <u>underlined</u> words into abbreviations.

1

Dear Gianni,

I am writing to tell you that I have gone to the beach with my sister Elena. I will be back this <u>evening</u>. Can you please water the plants?

Love

Carla

2

Dear Alex,

How are you? Your friend Marek phoned this <u>morning</u>. Would you please phone him back <u>as soon as possible</u> on this <u>telephone number</u>: 4596351.

All the best,

Ania

3 Write notes for these situations.

0 Your friend Tina has gone shopping. You are meeting your friend Adam at the Robodex exhibition. You're going for a pizza with friends afterwards. You will phone Tina this afternoon.

Tina,

Meeting Adam at Robodex exhibition. Going for a pizza afterwards. Will phone this p.m.

Sophie

1 You've borrowed your sister Alba's backpack. You've gone to your friend Katie's house. You're coming back on Friday night.

2 You have gone to the gym. You will cook dinner when you get back. You want your flatmate Sam to get some coffee and some orange juice.

Body works

Grammar 1: *must, mustn't, have to, don't have to* ▶ CB page 59

About the language

must, mustn't, have to, don't have to

We use **must**, **mustn't** and **have to** to express strong obligation and necessity.

We use **don't have to** to express lack of obligation.

must
We use **must** to talk about obligations that come from the speaker. *Must* is often used for personal opinions.

*I **must** get some milk before the shops close.*

mustn't
We use **mustn't** to tell people **not** to do things.

*You **mustn't** say things like that to your father.*

have to
We use **have to** to talk about strong obligations that do not come from the speaker. *Have to* is often used for things that are outside the speaker's control.

*I **have to** wear glasses when I drive.*

don't have to
We use **don't have to** to talk about a lack of obligation in the present or future.

*I **don't have to** go to school tomorrow. It's a holiday.*

! Typical mistakes ∙∙∙∙∙∙∙∙∙∙∙∙∙∙∙

I must ~~to~~ get a new tennis racquet.

    mustn't
You ~~don't must~~ use your mobile phone in the library.

    don't have to
You ~~mustn't~~ train very hard to enjoy some sports.

1 Complete these sentences. Use *must* or *have to* and the verbs in the box.

   wear   write   take   meet up   ~~see~~   send

0 You ....**must see**.......... Spielberg's latest film. It's on at the Rex Cinema.

1 I .... Carla a card. It's her birthday next week.

2 We .... for a coffee sometime. I can't wait to hear all your news.

3 'You .... a crash helmet, even if you're only travelling a short distance,' said the police officer.

4 Sara .... a two-thousand-word essay for her history exam.

5 I .... these tablets three times a day for the next week.

2 Write sentences about these signs. Use *mustn't*.

0 *You mustn't smoke in the hospital.*...........

Do not walk on the grass

1 ....

Do not feed the animals

2 ....

Ⓟ No Parking

3 ....

4 ....

Ⓢ No football on the beach

5 ....

3 Tell someone else about these obligations. Use ... *says I have to ...* .

0 'You must wear a crash helmet,' said her father.

My father says I have to wear a crash helmet.

1 'And you must always be home before 11 p.m.,' he added.

....

2 'You must drink more water, especially when it's hot like this,' said the doctor.

....

3 'Eat lots of fruit and vegetables,' she added.

....

4 'You must brush your teeth after every meal,' said the dentist.

....

5 'And I want you to have a check-up every six months,' she added.

....

4 Underline the best alternative.

Mireia: I (0) *have to/must* remember to get tickets for *Chariots of Fire*. It's on at the Film Festival tomorrow night. The film guide says you (1) *have to/must* get there early to get a good seat.

Laurent: Why don't you phone and reserve some seats? That way, you (2) *don't have to/mustn't* get there until they open the doors to the cinema at eight o'clock. By the way, I (3) *have to/must* tell you who we saw there on Saturday. Bettina and Alberto!

Mireia: Do you think they're back together?

Laurent: It looks as if they are. Sorry, Mireia. There's someone at the door. I (4) *have to/must* go. Listen, we (5) *have to/must* get together soon.

Mireia: Yes, and you (6) *have to/must* tell me *everything* about Bettina and Alberto!

Grammar 2: Requests with *can*, *could* and *would* ▶ CB page 61

About the language

Requests with *can*, *could* and *would*

- We can make requests using *can, could* and *would*. *Could* and *would* are usually a little more polite than *can*.

  Can/Could I/you* + infinitive without *to

  Can I have a cheese sandwich, please?
  Could you write that down, please?

  Would you* + infinitive without *to

  Would you pass me the salt, please?

- We also use these words in indirect questions.

  Can/Could you tell me where the sports stadium is?
  Would you mind telling me where the nearest bank is?

- We can make positive responses to requests using:

  OK.   Yes, of course.   That's fine.   No problem.

  A: *Can I try these shoes on, please?*
  B: *Yes, of course.*

- The affirmative response to an indirect question or request with *Would you mind...?* is formed using the negative.

  A: *Would you mind telling me how to use the fax machine?*
  B: *Not at all.*

- When we make negative responses to requests, we usually give a reason.

  Sorry, I haven't finished reading it.
  Sorry, someone's sitting there.

> **! Typical mistakes**
>
> Can I ~~to~~ use your phone?
> Would you ~~to~~ make a copy of this letter?
> Could
> ~~Would~~ I borrow your dictionary?
>
> A: *Would you mind helping me move these books?*
> Not at all
> B: ~~Yes, I would.~~ *Where would you like to put them.*

1   Make polite requests. Use the verbs in the box.
The + tells you how polite your request should be.

| lend   slow down   phone   ~~speak up~~   close   get |
| tell   try on   write |

0   *Can you speak up* .... a bit? I can't hear what you're
saying. +

1   .... me five euros until tomorrow?
I forgot to go to the bank. +

2   .... You're driving much too fast. +

3   .... me tomorrow evening? I'll be at
home after eight o'clock. ++

4   .... these shoes in a size 37, please? +

5   .... the window? It's a little cold in
here. ++

6   .... that word on the board? I don't
think I know it. ++

7   .... a lift home with you? I haven't got
my car with me. ++

8   .... me where the post office is,
please? +

2   Put the words in order to make polite requests
with *would*.

0   please the time mind telling me you would ?
Would you mind telling me the time, please?
....

1   help please would you me boxes move these ?
....

2   Harcourt Avenue please take me would you to?
....

3   please late would tell you the teacher I am going to be that?
....

4   feed cats my would please you away while I am?
....

5   mind would telling you me bought where you your
t-shirt?
....

6   be quieter a bit please would you?
....

3   Match these mini dialogues to the
pictures and then complete the requests
and responses. There is one picture you
don't need to use.

a   ☐

b   ☐

c   ☐

d   ☐

1
Girl: (1) .... try
             this skirt on in blue, please?
Assistant: (2) .... ,
             we don't have it in blue.
Girl: Well, (3) ....
             try it on in brown then?
Assistant: (4) ....
             I'll just get you one.

2
Man: (5) .... give
             me some change for the phone?
Assistant: (6) .... ,
             I haven't got any two euro coins.
Man: OK. (7) ....
             have a ten euro phonecard, then?
Assistant: (8) ....
             Here you are.

3
Woman: (9) .... bring
             me two croissants and a white
             coffee, please?
Waiter: (10) .... We
             don't have any croissants this
             morning.
Woman: Well, (11) ....
             I have some toast, please?
Waiter: (12) .... I'll
             bring it right away.

4 Now write a dialogue in your notebook for the picture you didn't use in exercise 3. Use these prompts.

A: Request information about next train to Brighton.

B: Give information: express train at ten thirty and slow train at five past ten.

A: Request return ticket on express train.

B: Give passenger tickets and tell him how much they cost: £18.50.

Vocabulary 1: Sports ▶ *CB page 56*

1 Find words connected with sports in the wordsearch grid below and use them to complete this table. Some words can be used more than once.

tennis	....
athletics	....
motor racing	....
football	....
basketball	....

T	E	C	N	I	S	B	A	U	S	K
C	R	A	S	H	H	E	L	M	E	T
O	F	P	I	T	C	H	T	P	B	R
U	A	T	L	L	R	A	C	I	C	A
R	R	A	C	K	E	T	A	R	W	C
T	G	I	R	E	E	B	N	E	T	K
B	A	N	T	M	N	A	S	I	P	L

2 <u>Underline</u> the best alternative in these paragraphs.

There are four people (0) *in/on* a tennis court. They are playing a match. There are quite a lot of (1) *spectators/audience* watching them so it must be quite important. Perhaps it is the (2) *end/final* of a big tournament like Wimbledon.

This photo shows some people at a motor racing track. The (3) *pilot/driver* is getting ready for the next (4) *race/career*. He is getting in his car and (5) *putting/putting on* his helmet.

We can see a large stadium with three athletes and a man in a suit. The man is (6) *putting/giving* the athletes medals for coming first, second and third. It could be the European (7) *Championships/Prizes* or perhaps the Olympic Games.

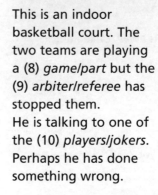

This is an indoor basketball court. The two teams are playing a (8) *game/part* but the (9) *arbiter/referee* has stopped them. He is talking to one of the (10) *players/jokers*. Perhaps he has done something wrong.

Vocabulary 2: Phrasal verbs (Health and fitness) ▶ *CB page 63*

1 Match the sentence halves.

0 If I eat tomatoes, I come ...

1 The camera wouldn't work because we hadn't carried ...

2 Several people passed ...

3 A lot of my friends have come ...

4 I don't know whether the citizens of Santa Cruz will ever get ...

5 The traffic, noise and pollution in this city are really getting me ...

6 You look completely worn ...

a) down. Let's move to the countryside.

b) out the instructions properly.

c) over the storm that hit the city on 31 March 2002.

d) out because it was so hot inside the tent.

e) down with that terrible flu I had.

f) out. Why don't you go to bed?

g) out in red spots all over my chest.

0 ..*g*..   1 ....   2 ....   3 ....   4 ....   5 ....   6 ....

2 Circle the alternative which is <u>not</u> possible to complete these sentences.

1 It took me a long time to get over ....

  A the boy I met last summer

  B the flu

  C doing so well in the exams

2 If you carry out my ...., nothing will go wrong.

  A ideas

  B instructions

  C orders

3 She came down with .... the night before the exams.

  A a nasty stomach bug

  B winning the lottery

  C flu

4 Everyone who ate the mushrooms came out in ....

  A a rash

  B spots

  C a fever

3 Read this extract from a letter and choose the correct word for each space. Circle your answer.

> Sorry I haven't been in touch for a while but I haven't been very well.
>
> I'm feeling quite (0) .... with all my college work and the pressure of exams is really (1) .... Also, I still haven't recovered from a nasty illness I got last week. I was walking to college last Monday when I suddenly felt faint and thought I was going to (2) .... I thought perhaps I (3) .... flu, so I got a taxi home. When I got home, I noticed that I (4) .... in a rash. There were little red spots all over my face and neck. My sister called the doctor when she came home. He said that I had food poisoning. He told me to stay in bed and to drink lots of water. He said that if I (5) .... his instructions, I would probably (6) .... in a few days, but I still feel quite weak.

0 Ⓐ worn out   B worn over   C worn in

1 A getting me down
  B getting down me
  C having me down

2 A pass over   B pass through   C pass out

3 A was coming out with
  B was coming down with
  C was coming over with

4 A was coming out
  B was coming over
  C was coming out

5 A carried over   B carried out
  C carried through

6 A get it over   B get over it   C get with it

Listening

1 You are going to hear snowboard champion Shannon Dunn talking about her life in sport. Look at the types of information in the list and match them to the gaps in the notes.

a) an amount of money ☐

b) a place ☐

c) a period of time ☐

d) a part of the body ☐

e) a family member ☐

f) an activity or sport ☐

Grew up in (1) .... and Steamboat, Colorado

Started snowboarding with her (2) .... Sean

Parents gave both children $ (3) .... for snowboarding tour

Parents' attitude: encouraging

Shannon on competition 'It isn't as important as having fun'

Spends summers (4) ....

Most important part of body for snowboarding: (5) ....

Most important part of body for surfing: upper body

Time spent at home each year: (6) ....

2 Now listen and fill in the missing information.

Speaking

1 Listen to two students discussing the photographs below. Which student, the boy or the girl, asks for the other person's opinion? ....

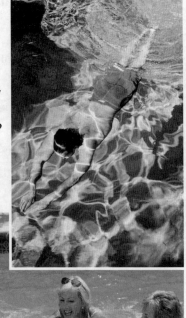

2 Listen again and complete the conversation by filling in the gaps.

Josue: I (0) .... *think* .... water aerobics would be a lot of fun,
(1) ....?

Nadia: I'm not sure. I've never tried it.

Josue: No, I haven't tried it either, but they seem to be having a great time jumping around in the water. It looks like a mixture of swimming and aerobics. I like aerobics and I love swimming.
(2) ....?

Nadia: I like swimming alone like that.

Josue: Yes, I like to swim alone sometimes too. What other kinds of exercises
(3) ....?

Nadia: Jogging and skiing.

3 Add expressions for asking someone's opinion to what Nadia says. Write your answers in your notebook.

Nadia: I'm not sure. I've never tried it. *What about you?*

Writing: Informal letters and punctuation ▶ *Writing Reference page 148*

1 Here are some examples from students' writing. Each student has a particular punctuation problem. Match the examples to the punctuation problems.

a) commas ☐

b) apostrophes ☐

c) capital letters ☐

d) full stops ☐

e) direct speech ☐

1

One of the most interesting places in my city is the old town it was built in the sixteenth century and it is still there today when you come here you must visit it

2

Most of the tourists who come here are english and they don't usually understand very much spanish. my friend jenny does though. she did a course at the university of salamanca last year

3

I'm going to Venice Florence Pisa and Rome. If I have time I want to visit Naples too. Rosaria the girl I met in Bristol last summer lives there.

4

Watch out! You're going to drop those plates shouted my mother, but it was too late. I'd already dropped them.

5

My cousins favourite sport is basketball. Shes got photos of players from the top teams all over her bedroom wall. She doesnt play basketball herself, though

2 Correct their mistakes.

3 Look at this email message and underline the alternative which is not appropriate.

Hi/Dear/Bye Tony,

How are you?/How do you do?/How are things?

What a surprise!/Guess what?/You'll never believe this! I'm coming to Verona next month and Lucca is coming with me. We'll phone you and arrange to meet up. *I can't wait to/It'll be fantastic to/I am looking forward to* see you again!

Finally/Anyway/So, send me a message soon!

Love/Lots of love/Yours faithfully,

Gloria

4 Write an email message to a friend. Use the prompts below and the message in exercise 3 to give you ideas.

• Start your message with an informal greeting.
• Ask your friend how s/he is.
• Tell him/her that you have some surprising news.
• Tell him/her what it is.
• Say that you are pleased about it.
• Ask him/her to send you a message.
• Finish your message with an informal greeting.

UNIT

8 Lifestyle

Grammar 1: Present perfect simple (for indefinite past) ▶ *CB page 65*

About the language

Present perfect simple

- We use the present perfect simple (*have/has* + past participle) to talk about things that have happened at some time in our lives when the time that the action happened is indefinite (unknown or unimportant).

   *I've **been** to Scotland but I **haven't been** to Ireland.*

- We usually use *ever, never, already, yet* and *just* with the present perfect.

   *Have you **ever** been sailing?*
   *I've **never** eaten snails.*
   *I've **already** decided that I am going to get a boat when I'm older.*
   *We haven't bought her a present **yet**.*
   *Have you thought about it **yet**?*
   *He's **just** made his bed.*

- When we mention a finished time in the past we use the past simple.

   *I've already seen that film. I **saw** it **last Saturday**.*

   A: *Have you ever seen a whale?*
   B: *Yes. I **saw** one once **when we were on holiday** in New Zealand.*

- With the verb *go* we use **has/have gone** when the person is still there and we use **has/have been** when the person has returned.

   *I've **been** to the United States three times. He's **gone** to Paris. He'll be back next week.*

> **Typical mistakes**
>
> ~~been to~~
> *Have you ever ~~gone to~~ Finland?*
> *Have you been (ever) camping?*
> *(Never) she's liked meat.*
> *She's liked meat (never).*
> *(Already) I've cooked the dinner.*
> *We (yet) haven't done the shopping.*
> *Have you (yet) finished reading it?*
> *(Yet) have you finished reading it?*
> *He (just) has come back from Greece.*
> *never*
> *She has ~~n't ever~~ met my brother.*

---

1 Use the prompts to make sentences or questions with the present perfect simple.

0 you / see / the new Johnny Depp film?

   Have you seen the new Johnny Depp film?

1 I / see / all of the films that won Oscars.

   ....

2 She / visit / France, Italy and Spain.

   ....

3 She / not travel / anywhere outside Europe.

   ....

4 they / ever try / snowboarding?

   ....

5 you / ever eat / frogs' legs?

   ....

6 you / ever ride / a camel or an elephant?

   ....

2 Put the adverbs in the correct position in the sentences in this conversation.

Gustavo: (0) Have you *ever* been surfing? (ever)

Marina: (1) No, I've watched other people surfing lots of times, but I've been surfing myself. (never). What about you?

Gustavo: (2) No, I have tried it either (never), but I've decided I'm going to learn. (3) I've bought a surfboard. (already).

Marina: Wow! (4) How did you know what kind of board to buy if you haven't had any lessons (yet)?

Gustavo: (5) Well, I've talked to lots of surfers and looked at hundreds of boards in surfshops. (already)

Marina: (6) Have you bought a wetsuit (already)? The water here can be very cold even in the summer.

Gustavo: (7) It hasn't seemed particularly cold to me (ever). I suppose it would, though, if you were in there for a few hours instead of a few minutes.

3 Underline the best alternative in each sentence.

0 Have you *ever*/never met a famous sports or pop star?

1 I've *yet/already* seen the new Brad Pitt film. Can we go and see something else?

2 Sonia has *ever/never* slept in a tent before, so she's a bit anxious about the camping trip.

3 Haven't you finished washing the car *already/yet*? We're supposed to go out in about twenty minutes.

4 A: Can you phone Charlotte and tell her we're going to be late.
  B: I've *yet/already* phoned her.

5 I've *ever/never* met a girl like you before.

6 Tina hasn't written to Tom *already/yet* although she promised she would.

7 I've *just/yet* cleaned the floor so don't walk on it!

8 A: Have you been to the supermarket *just/yet*?
  B: No, not *just/yet*. I've *just/yet* got home from college.

4 Underline the correct verb form, past simple or present perfect.

A: (0) *Have you ever eaten/Did you ever eat* frogs' legs?
B: Yes, I have.

A: When (1) *have you eaten/did you eat* them?
B: I (2) *have had/had* them in a French restaurant a couple of years ago.

A: (3) *Have you liked/Did you like* them?
B: Well, I (4) *have eaten/ate* worse things.

A: What is the most disgusting thing you (5) *have ever eaten/ever ate*?
B: I don't know but my father (6) *has eaten/ate* snake once when he was in Australia.

5 Complete this letter using the correct form of the verbs in brackets.

Dear Marina,

I'm writing to you from Sydney, Australia. We (0) (arrive) __arrived__ last Thursday but I (1) (not write) .... to many of my friends back home yet, in fact you're the first!

We (2) (already do) .... lots of exciting things and I (3) (take) .... loads of photos. We (4) (go) .... to the top of one of the tallest buildings in Sydney, for a ferry trip and for a lovely drive out into the countryside.

Yesterday we (5) (go) .... to Tooronga Park Zoo. It was fantastic. I (6) (never see) .... so many fascinating animals!

We (7) (not go) .... to the famous Sydney Opera House yet, but Mum (8) (manage) .... to get tickets for a concert there tomorrow night. I can't wait.

I'll write again soon and tell you all about it.

Love,

Tania

Grammar 2: Present perfect simple (for unfinished past) ▶ CB page 70

About the language

Present perfect simple

- We use the present perfect simple to describe situations that have continued from some time in the past until now. We use *for* when we are talking about how long something has lasted. We use *since* when we are talking about when something started.

  My cousins **have lived** on a boat **for fifteen years**.
  I **haven't seen** Carlos **since April**.
  How long **have you known** Bea?

! Typical mistakes

   have lived
We ~~live~~ in Rome since 1987.

   have known
I ~~am knowing~~ Carlos for ten years.

1 Use the prompts to make sentences in the present perfect simple.

0 I / know Bea / six years.

I've known Bea for six years.

1 I / not see / her / a couple of weeks.

....

2 She / be / away on holiday / the beginning of August.

....

3 How long / Bea / live / in Madrid?

....

4 She / live / there / the beginning of 2002.

....

5 you / ever / share a flat / with her?

....

6 We / only / share / a flat / a month.

....

7 We / know / each other / much longer.

....

8 I / meet / her family and her boyfriend.

....

2 The Wilkinson family lives aboard a boat. Read and complete this text about them. Use the verbs in the box.

stop	learn	~~live~~	have	say
		do	visit	

The Wilkinsons built their boat in 1988. They (0) .... *have lived* .... aboard ever since. They started to sail around the world in 1999. So far they (1) .... France, Spain and Brazil. They usually stay in a port or marina for a couple of weeks. In the last year they (2) .... at twenty different cities and towns. Their children, Sunny and Jeffrey, meet people from all over the world. They (3) .... some French, Spanish and some Portuguese.

Of course they can't go to a normal school. Since they started sailing they (4) .... all their school work aboard *The Seagull*.

Every time they stop somewhere, the Wilkinsons make new friends, but Sunny thinks that she (5) .... 'goodbye' to too many people. Both Sunny and Jeffrey think there are disadvantages to living aboard but they (6) .... some fantastic experiences.

3 Complete the second sentence so that it is similar in meaning to the first sentence.

1 When did you start living in Verona?

How long ....?

2 The last time I saw Simon was in August.

I haven't ....

3 I met Simon ten years ago.

I have ....

4 This is my third visit to Greece.

I have ....

5 Is this your first trip to Europe?

Have you ....?

Vocabulary 1: House and home
▶ *CB page 66*

1 Use the words and phrases in the box to label the picture.

> garage   front door   fence   roof   gate
> drive   front garden   path   chimney

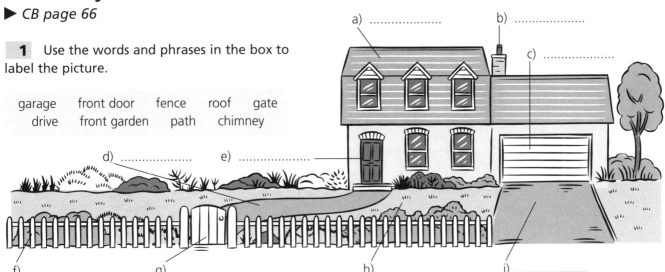

a) .... b) .... c) ....

d) .... e) ....

f) .... g) .... h) .... i) ....

2 Use phrases from the boxes to answer the questions.

1 Where do you park your motorbike?

> the corner of my street   the garage
> my friend's house

I usually park it …

in ....

on ....

outside ....

2 Where do your friends live?

> a block of flats   the ground floor   a boat

They live …

in ....

on ....

on ....

3 Where are you going to plant those flowers?

> the path   the front garden   the gate

I thought I would plant them …

along ....

next to ....

in ....

Vocabulary 2: Adjectives ending in *-ed/-ing*
▶ *CB page 71*

Read this letter. The student who wrote it has made some mistakes with *-ed/-ing* adjectives. Find the mistakes and correct them.

Dear Kamil,

I was really ~~pleasing~~ *pleased* to get your letter. It sounds like you are having a very busy time at college. I've been very busy too and I'm really looking forward to the holidays because I'm very tiring.

You wanted some information about Copenhagen and Cracow. Both cities are very interesting places to visit. There are quite a lot of similarities but there are also some important differences.

The weather can be very cold in Copenhagen and in Cracow, as I am sure you know. In winter the days are very short and this can be a bit depressed. Fortunately there are lots of things to do in both cities. I don't think you will ever be bored.

In Cracow there are a lot of places to go to listen to music and there are also a lot of cinemas. There is a wonderful museum, which I found absolutely fascinated. Copenhagen has lots to offer as well. There are wonderful cafés and the nightlife is really exciting too.

I hope that helps you make up your mind. It's a difficult decision. I won't be at all surprising if I hear you've decided to visit both cities.

All the best,

Gustavo

Reading

1 You are going to read an article about the Wilkinson family. Scan the article once quickly and answer these questions. Which member of the Wilkinson family (Mary, Sunny or Jeffrey) mentions the following?

1 learning languages
2 exams
3 the environment
4 dolphins and whales
5 friends

Living aboard

In many of the world's cities, on canals and rivers or in marinas, you can find people who have chosen to live on the water. The Wilkinsons have lived aboard their boat for fifteen years. Much of that time they have spent sailing around the world. Here's what they had to say about living aboard.

Mary Wilkinson

People sometimes ask me if I think it's fair to the children. How could it not be fair? They live in a less polluted, safer environment. They get to travel and become comfortable with and able to deal with people of all ages and from different cultures. This makes them confident and relaxed. Children who live aboard are often better educated because instead of being taught in overcrowded classrooms they learn with their brothers and sisters and with a parent as the teacher.

Sunny Wilkinson

People usually don't believe we live on a boat until I show them a photo. It seems so different to the lifestyles they know.

Of course living aboard has its advantages and disadvantages. It's fantastic living so close to nature and getting to know other cultures and languages.

It's also really exciting to sail off somewhere and know that you will see new places and meet new people, but sometimes I have made new friends somewhere and then they move on or we do. Saying goodbye to people is always hard.

Jeffrey Wilkinson

I've already decided that I'm going to get a boat when I'm older and go cruising with my friends. I have had so many experiences and seen so many amazing things: dolphins, whales, fantastic tropical fish and a lot of beautiful places on land as well. My only worry is how I will get on with the kids in a normal classroom and with the school system in general. I want to go to university and I don't know how well I'll do in the final exams. Mum and Dad both say I'm ahead of other kids of my age, but I'm not so sure.

2 Now read the article again and choose the best alternative to answer the questions.

1 What does the writer of the article want to tell her readers about?
   A One family's experience of living on a boat.
   B Why she thinks it's a good idea to live on a boat.
   C The disadvantages of living on a boat.
   D Where you can see people living on boats.

2 How does Mary Wilkinson feel about other lifestyles?
   A She thinks they are unfair to children.
   B She thinks they do not offer the advantages of living aboard.
   C She is not sure what she thinks about them.
   D She thinks they are safer than living aboard.

3 What is the main disadvantage of living aboard according to Sunny Wilkinson?
   A She has to learn foreign languages.
   B She hasn't made many friends.
   C They stay in the same place for too long.
   D She misses her friends.

4 Why is Jeffrey Wilkinson worried?
   A He does not know as much as other people his age.
   B His parents think he is behind other people his age.
   C He thinks he might not get good enough results to get into university.
   D He wants to go to a normal school.

5 Which of the Wilkinsons have the same opinions about the advantages of living aboard.
   A Mary and Jeffrey agree that the children are better educated.
   B Jeffrey and Sunny agree that meeting new people and getting to know new cultures are important.
   C Mary and Sunny agree that it is good to get away from pollution.
   D Sunny and Jeffrey both think it is wonderful to be in close contact with nature.

6 Which of the Wilkinsons mention positive and negative things about living aboard?
   A Sunny, but not Jeffrey or Mary.
   B Jeffrey, but not Sunny or Mary.
   C Mary, Jeffrey and Sunny.
   D Jeffrey and Sunny, but not Mary.

3 Find the following in the text:

1 a noun meaning small areas of water near the sea where people keep boats ....

2 an adjective meaning dirty and dangerous (air, water, land) ....

3 an adjective meaning that you are sure you can do something well ....

4 an adjective meaning with too many people ....

5 a phrasal verb meaning to go away to another place ....

6 a phrasal verb meaning to have a good relationship with ....

7 an adjective meaning more successful than someone ....

Writing: Transactional letter and linkers of contrast ▶ *Writing Reference page 150*

1 Put the sections of this letter into the correct order.

1 ..*i*. 2 ...... 3 ...... 4 ...... 5 ...... 6 ...... 7 ......

8 ...... 9 ......

Dear Jeffrey,

a) So, that's all my news.

b) It was good to hear that you and the rest of the family are enjoying life at sea. It really does sound amazing!

c) So, you want to know about Paris. It's a very beautiful city but it can be expensive, especially food and drinks.

d) I'm sure you've got lots more really exciting things to tell me about crossing the Atlantic and Brazil, so write soon.

e) Public transport, on the other hand, is much cheaper than it is in London and very efficient.

f) This, however, was not very good for our French.

g) People were very helpful and didn't seem to mind giving directions in English at all!

h) Although everyone says the French don't like speaking English, that wasn't our impression.

i) Thanks for your letter.

Lots of love,

Charlotte

2   The letter should have four paragraphs. Decide which sentences go into each paragraph.

Paragraph 1: ....*i*........   Paragraph 3: ....

Paragraph 2: ....   Paragraph 4: ....

Linkers

Linker	Use	Position
but	to add something different or surprising	between two parts of sentence
however	to emphasise that something is different or surprising	at the beginning or at the end of the sentence
although	to say things are surprising or different to what we expect	at the beginning of the part of the sentence without the surprising thing
on the other hand	to make a contrast with information in the previous sentence	at the beginning or in the middle of the new sentence

3   <u>Underline</u> the correct linker in these sentences.

0   I love the village where I live <u>*but*</u>/*on the other hand* sometimes I miss the excitement of a big city.

1   The peace and quiet of the countryside is wonderful, *on the other hand/although* it is sometimes spoilt by tourists speeding through in their noisy cars.

2   Last year, I decided to move to a bigger town. *However/Although*, when I saw how expensive the houses were there, I changed my mind.

3   The food from our village shop is absolutely delicious. *Although/On the other hand* it is considerably more expensive than food from the supermarket in town.

4   *Although/However* our village is twenty miles from the nearest big town, the bus service is very bad.

5   It's not an ideal life in the country. *But/However*, despite all its faults, I'm still very glad that I decided to stay in the village.

4   Match the two sentences and rewrite each pair as one sentence in your notebook, using a linker.

0   The days are incredibly short in Helsinki in December.

1   The trains were very expensive.

2   We left for the airport in plenty of time.

3   There is a very efficient bus service on the island.

4   The streets were quite crowded during the day.

5   The food in the seaside restaurants is excellent.

a) We still missed the plane.

b) They were very dirty and didn't run on time.

c) ~~In summer it doesn't get dark until late at night.~~

d) There was no nightlife at all that we could find.

e) The service is very poor.

f) We chose to hire a car.

0   *The days are incredibly short in Helsinki in December. In the summer, on the other hand, it doesn't get dark until late at night.*

5   Rewrite this letter in your notebook, using some of the linkers from the box in exercise 2.

Dear Fiodr

Thank you so much for your letter. I am pleased to hear about your new girlfriend. It's sad that things didn't work out between you and Tanya.

The house looks wonderful now. It took us a very long time to finish all the decorating. It was worth all the effort! Sometimes I think we should have used a professional decorator - it would have saved us so much work. It would have cost us a lot more money!

Ulrike has started school now. She was nervous about her first day. She was very excited to be starting at 'proper' school. I felt a little sad saying goodbye to her. I'm enjoying the extra free time at home.

Do write back and tell me all your news. And send a photograph of your new girlfriend!

All the best

Andrea

More than words

Grammar 1: Defining relative clauses ▶
CB page 73

About the language

Defining relative clauses

- We use defining relative clauses to define or identify a noun. They tell us exactly which person, thing, time or place we are talking about. No commas are used.

  *Gregoria Alonso is the woman **who** has moved into the house next door.*

  *She's the woman **whose** son plays in a rock band.*

  *What's the name of the island **where** they 'talk' by whistling?*

  *1984 was the year **when** I left London.*

  *Here's the book **which** Bea lent me.*

- We can use *that* instead of *who, which* or *when*.

  *This is the shop **that** I told you about.*
  *This is the dictionary **that** the teacher recommended.*
  *1969 was the year **that** people first walked on the moon.*

- *Whose* is used for people and things.

  *That's the house **whose** roof fell in.*

- When *who, which* etc. is the <u>object</u> of the verb you can leave it out of the sentence.

                  object   object
  Bea read <u>several books</u> that summer. <u>The book</u> (which/that) she read about the Canary Islands was very interesting.

! Typical mistakes

That's the hotel/where we stayed last year.
That's the boy who I told you about ~~him~~.
She's the girl that ~~she~~ likes me.

---

1 Match the first halves of the sentences to the second halves.

0 Wednesday is the day

1 Nayra is the member of my family

2 'Beautiful' is the perfume

3 'Noctua' is the name of the discotheque

4 I can't remember the name of the song

5 Nayra says the group

a) when my sister Nayra is coming home.

b) that made the record are coming here next month.

c) that was playing that night.

d) who I get on with best.

e) where she met her boyfriend.

f) which Nayra likes to wear.

0 ..*a*.. 1 ...... 2 ...... 3 ...... 4 ...... 5 ......

2 Tania is visiting the place where she grew up. Choose the correct relative pronouns from the box to complete her sentences.

> which   where   who   when
>   whose

0 'That's the house ...*where*... we used to live.'

1 'And there's the school .... I used to go to.'

2 'And that's Obdulia. She's the woman .... daughter was my best friend.'

3 'She's the girl .... I ran away with.'

4 'Hermigua was the village .... they found us.'

5 '1966 was the year .... we ran away.'

3   Put the words in order to make sentences with defining relative clauses.

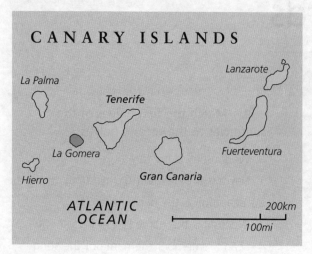

0   about book is the people communicate who by whistling.

   The book is about people who communicate by whistling.

1   La Gomera one of the places whistling language use they where is

   ....

2   our holidays is also we go for it where

   ....

3   when August the month is go there usually we

   ....

4   Stelios the boy who is Greek met I there summer last

   ....

5   the one he is brother whose plays for Newcastle United

   ....

6   team won the championship that Newcastle United were not the

   ....

4   Tick (✓) the sentences where it is possible to leave out the relative pronoun.

1   We've got two cats that we've had since they were kittens.

2   Sam is the one that you can see in the photo.

3   Max is the one that sleeps in this basket.

4   This ball is the toy that Max likes to play with.

5   *Pettreat* is the only brand of cat food that they will eat.

6   *Coombes* is the only supermarket that sells *Pettreat*.

7   Sunday is the day that *Coombes* is closed.

Grammar 2: Non-defining relative clauses
▶ *CB page 77*

About the language

Non-defining relative clauses

- We use **non-defining relative clauses** to give extra information. They tell us more about a person, thing, time or place that is already identified.

- Commas are used before and after the relative clause.

- Non-defining relative clauses are generally more formal and more common in writing.

- We don't usually use *that* in non-defining relative clauses.

   *Busselton, **where my friend Lily lives**, is in Western Australia.*

   *In August, **when my father has his holidays**, we are all going to La Gomera.*

   *Liam, **who has just walked in**, is the boy my sister is going out with.*

   *I read Stephen King's latest book, **which I found absolutely terrifying**.*

Typical mistakes

Budapest⊙where my cousins live ⊙ is one of my favourite cities.

1   Decide if these sentences contain defining or non-defining relative clauses. Mark them D or ND.

1   My mother, who went to a French school, still speaks French with her sisters. ☐

2   My father always speaks to us in Greek, which is his first language. ☐

3   That's the International School where I studied. ☐

4   The International Baccalaureat is an examination that many students take at the end of school. ☐

5   Medicine, which is what I am studying, is a very demanding degree course. ☐

6   Dr Divasson is the teacher whose classes I enjoy most. ☐

2   Punctuate these sentences.

0   My friend Clara ① who I met in England ① is from Barcelona.

1   To celebrate her birthday which is next week we are all going out for a pizza.

2   Pizzeria Da Canio where we went for my birthday last year as well is not very expensive.

3   In September when Clara will be in Dublin I might go and visit her.

4   The family she is going to stay with who have twin daughters called Maeve and Sinead is really nice.

5   Trinity College, Dublin where Maeve and Sinead are studying has a special course for students of English as a foreign language.

6   At Christmas when Clara goes back to Barcelona Maeve and Sinead are going to organise a big farewell party for her.

3   Join the following sentences to make one sentence with a non-defining relative clause.

0   Billy Wilder was one of Hollywood's most famous film directors and writers. He was not a native speaker of English.

Billy Wilder, who was not a native speaker of English, was one of Hollywood's most famous film directors and writers.

1   His English was not very good when he arrived in the United States. He had learnt all his English from listening to songs.

....

....

2   *Some Like it Hot* is one of his best-known films. It starred Marilyn Monroe.

....

....

3   Billy Wilder shared a room with an actor called Peter Laurie. He was also trying to find work.

....

....

4   Eventually Peter Laurie became very famous. He was in the film *Casablanca*.

....

....

5   By 2002 Billy Wilder had written more than seventy films. Billy Wilder died then.

....

....

Vocabulary 1: Sounds ▶ *CB page 74*

Complete this story with words from the box.

> screaming   slammed   ringing   bang
> ~~yawning~~   whistling   whispering
> sneezed   shouting

A tiring day

I felt very tired that day. I couldn't stop (0) *__yawning__* in class and my eyes kept closing. Some boys in the back row were (1) .... and our teacher was getting very annoyed.

I realised that I was starting to get a cold and decided to take the bus home. I must have (2) .... about fifty times on the way home. I got home and made myself a cup of tea. Then I heard someone (3) .... the doorbell. It was one of my neighbours. She looked very worried. She explained that she had lost her dog. I told her that I hadn't seen it and I went to bed. Outside I could hear my neighbour (4) .... 'Here Fluffy!' and (5) .... to it.

I was beginning to fall asleep when I heard a woman (6) .... and then there was a loud (7) .... as if someone had (8) .... a door. I was about to call the police when I realised that it was my neighbours' TV!

Vocabulary 2: Phrasal verbs (Communication) ▶ *CB page 78*

1   Complete this conversation. Use the correct form of the phrasal verbs in the box.

> shut up   look up   make up   tell off
> get through to   catch on   speak up

Roberto: I've been trying to (1) .... Tania all day but her phone's switched off.

Athena: I phoned her this morning when I was on the bus. She couldn't hear me very well and she asked me to (2) .... In the end I was shouting and a very rude man opposite me told me to (3) .... I couldn't believe it!

Roberto: What? A complete stranger. Are you (4) .... stories again, Athena?

Athena: No, it's true. He was really angry.

Roberto: Mobile phones do annoy some people. Mine rang in class yesterday. The teacher really (5) .... me .... for forgetting to switch it off. She was trying to explain something very complex.

Athena: What was that?

Roberto: I don't know. I asked Gloria afterwards. She's really intelligent and usually (6) .... to everything the teacher explains, but she seemed really confused as well.

Athena: Well, I suggest you (7) .... it .... in the Grammar Reference. You never know, she might put it in the exam.

2   Circle the alternative that is <u>not</u> possible in these sentences.

1   Could you put me through to ....?
    A the manager's office   B extension 197
    C here

2   She makes up really funny ....
    A clothes   B stories   C jokes

3   The teacher told them off ....
    A because they were talking   B for talking
    C to talk

4   I don't always catch on ....
    A about maths   B to Susanna's jokes
    C straight away

5   I always have to look up ....
    A my friend's phone number   B my brother
    C that word in the dictionary

3 Complete the responses to these comments and questions. Use the phrasal verbs from exercise 1.

0 A: You've been trying to avoid me.

   B: That's not true! I've been trying to ....*get through to*............ you all day.

1 A: Was he telling the truth when he said he used to live in California?

   B: No, he was just .... it .... to impress you.

2 A: Can you remember all your friends' phone numbers?

   B: No, I have to .... them .... in my address book.

3 A: Did the teacher tell them to keep still?

   B: No she told them to .... because they kept talking.

4 A: I hope I wasn't speaking too loud.

   B: Not at all. I was going to ask you to .... because I couldn't hear you properly.

5 A: Pavlos doesn't seem to have much of a sense of humour. I've never heard him tell a joke.

   B: No, but he .... very quickly when someone else tells one.

6 A: Did your mother thank you for looking after your little brother?

   B: No, she .... for not taking him to the park.

Reading

1 You are going to read an article about how four people learnt another language. Read it through once quickly and answer this question.

Which language did each person learn?

1 Janna ....

2 Liam ....

3 Clare ....

4 Tom ....

Janna

I went to classes at a language school when I first got there, but they weren't very good. We did lots of grammar and not much else. Eventually, I realised that I could learn better on my own. I started by listening to the news on the radio in English and then reading about the same stories in an Italian newspaper. After a while I started to try and read about things that hadn't been on the radio news and then I actually tried to read a novel, which I'd already read in English. After only six months I could read quite difficult things without having to look up too many words in the dictionary.

Liam

It was music that made me want to learn Spanish in the first place. I just wanted to be able to understand the words. Of course I had been listening to Spanish songs for years and I even sang in Spanish with a group of friends. However, I didn't really understand what I was singing about. One day at the end of one of our performances, a girl came up and started speaking to me in Spanish. I was really embarrassed because I had to tell her I couldn't understand her. She offered to teach me. Now I speak it quite well and I sing in it even better!

Clare

When I first met Laurent, we used to speak to each other in English. He didn't mind but I thought it was unfair that he always had to speak in a foreign language, especially since it was because my French really wasn't good enough. Apart from that, whenever we had an argument, he would lose because he didn't know how to be angry in English. After we moved to Paris, my French got better and we always spoke it when we went out with friends. It was quite hard for me at first because suddenly I was the one who always had to speak in a foreign language. Now we even speak it at home quite a lot.

Tom

It was a fantastic opportunity to go and play for a Japanese team. There was only one small problem: the club said I would have to learn Japanese. They arranged for me to be taught one-to-one. I lived in the teacher's house for a month before the team started training. We spoke Japanese all day, from when we got up in the morning till when we went to bed at night, so we talked about all sorts of different things. Luckily we got on very well but it was very tiring and hard for me. I've still got a lot to learn but by the end of that first month I could communicate.

2   Now read the texts again and answer these questions.

Which of the people:

0 went to a school to learn the language?   *Janna*

1 found the experience of learning the language difficult?   ....

....

2 had used the language before they started learning it?   ....

3 was told they had to learn the language?   ....

4 was not happy with the way they were taught?   ....

5 learnt the language on their own?   ....

6 says how long it took them to learn to use the language?   ....

....

7 had private lessons?   ....

....

8 has a boyfriend or girlfriend who speaks English and another language?   ....

Speaking: Comparing two photographs

1   Look at the four photographs and listen to a student comparing two of them. Which two photographs does she compare?

2   Listen again and fill in the gaps in these sentences.

1 Well, ... these photographs are about communication.

2 .... I can see a person reading a book.

3 The other photograph .... an important international meeting.

4 .... they are quite different, the two photographs .... because they both show people communicating in special ways.

3   Now listen for a third time and complete these phrases.

1 but the book is writing, ... written in a special language

2 I'm not sure .... in English.

3 the Nations ...., the United Nations.

4 What's the word? .... you put on your ears ....

4   Use these prompts to write a description in your notebook of the other two photographs.

both photographs/learning languages

first one/see/students in language laboratory
they/wearing ....
not/sure/what/called/English
but/think/might be/'headphones'
the students/listening/cassette/or/instructor

other photograph/see/chimpanzee
seem/learn/sign language
because/instructor/making/sign

although/different/similar

because/both chimpanzee and students/
listening carefully

Writing: Discursive composition ▶
Writing Reference page 156

1   Look at this task and the notes a student has made. Tick (✓) the advantages and cross (✗) the disadvantages.

> Your class have been discussing the idea of studying English in an English-speaking country. Your teacher has asked you to write a composition summarising the main points of your discussion in 110–130 words.

1   lots of opportunities to use English outside class ☐

2   get to know English-speaking people ☐

3   expensive ☐

4   miss friends and family ☐

5   learn about another culture ☐

6   easy to get English books, records, videos etc. ☐

7   difficult to get used to food ☐

8   many schools have extra activities (museum visits, day trips to famous places etc.) ☐

9   weather can be very cold in some English-speaking countries, even in summer ☐

2   Look at the two plans, A and B, for the composition task. Which one is a good plan?

A

> *Introduction*
> Most people think it's a good idea to go to an English-speaking country
>
> *Main Section*
> • lots of opportunities to use English outside class
> • get to know English-speaking people
> • get to know another culture
> • easy to get English books, records, videos etc.
>
> *Conclusion:*
> Summary of opinion: Doesn't matter which English-speaking country, it's a good idea.

3   This is what another student wrote in her composition. She has not used any linking expressions for addition (*also ...; as well as that ...; in addition ...*). Rewrite her composition in your notebook, including these linking expressions.

> Most people think there are more advantages than disadvantages in going to an English-speaking country to study.
> Firstly, you have lots of opportunities to use English outside class. You get to know English-speaking people. You learn about another culture. It will be easy to get English books, records and videos, which you can use when you go back to your country.
> In conclusion, it doesn't matter which English-speaking country you choose to study in, there will be many good reasons to go there and improve your English.

Most people think there are more advantages than disadvantages in going to an English-speaking country to study.
Firstly, you have lots of opportunities to use English outside class. Also, you get to know English-speaking people.

4   Now write a paragraph in your notebook about the disadvantages of going to study in an English-speaking country. Use the points from exercise 1 and the linking expressions you used in exercise 3.

B

> People mainly in favour of studying in English-speaking countries
> My opinion – not such a good idea. It's too expensive

Grammar 1: Conditionals (1) ▶ *CB page 83*

About the language

Zero conditional

Form

If + present + present in the main clause

Use

To say what always happens.

If you **sit** *on that chair, the cat* **jumps** *onto your knee.*

First conditional

Form

If + present simple + *will* for future in the main clause

Use

To describe what may possibly happen.

If you **don't train** *hard enough, you* **won't win.**

Second conditional

Form

If + past simple + *would, could* etc. in the main clause

Use

To talk about something:

- that is impossible and just imagined.

 If **I was** *a dog, I* **would refuse** *to eat dog food.*

- which is very unlikely to happen in the future.

 If we **went** *to live on a boat, we* **would be able** *to take our cat with us.*

> **! Typical mistakes** ••••••••••••••••••
>
> *If we ~~will~~ have enough money, we will be able to go to Italy this summer.*
>
> *will*
> *If I have enough time, I ∧visit Carla next time I am in Rome.*
>
> *didn't*
> *If Lucy ~~wouldn't~~ feel better, she wouldn't be going away.*
>
> *would spend*
> *If they had somewhere to stay in London, they ~~spent~~ at least a week there.*

1 Combine the sentences to make zero conditionals with *if*.

0 I don't have anything to do on Saturday morning. I stay in bed until 10 o'clock.

 If I don't have anything to do on Saturday morning, I stay in bed until 10 o'clock.

1 I have a basketball match. I get up much earlier.

 ....

 ....

2 It's a sunny morning. I walk to the sports club.

 ....

 ....

3 It's raining. My sister drives me.

 ....

 ....

4 She's not busy. She stays to watch the match.

 ....

 ....

5 Our team wins. We all go out for lunch to celebrate.

 ....

2   Complete these sentences with the correct form of the verbs in brackets.

0   If I .... *pass* .... my exams, my parents .... *will buy* .... me a motorbike. (pass, buy)

1   If Sarah .... more money, she .... in a bigger house. (have, live)

2   We .... late if you .... a bit faster! (not be, drive)

3   If I .... a bad cold, I .... hot water with lemon and ginger. (have, drink)

4   George .... in the south of France if he .... a job there. (live, get)

5   If Jamie .... coffee in the morning, he .... sleepy all day. (not drink, feel)

6   My teacher .... very angry if I .... my homework again. (be, forget)

3   Complete these sentences with the correct form of the verbs in brackets.

0   How .... *do you feel* .... (feel) if you don't get enough sleep?

1   What would you say if you .... (meet) someone really famous?

2   Who do you talk to if you .... (be) worried about something.

3   How .... (feel) if Australia won the next World Cup?

4   How do you keep in touch with Mike if .... (not have) his email?

5   What .... (do) if you failed your exams this year?

6   What .... (happen) if Celtic Rangers wins the match tonight?

4   Match the questions from exercise 3 to these answers.

a) They'll play in the European Cup in June. ☐

b) Pretty terrible. I need at least seven hours. ☐ *0*

c) Take some extra lessons during the holiday. ☐

d) My sister. ☐

e) Very surprised! ☐

f) I phone him every Friday afternoon. ☐

g) 'Hello, my name's Simon.' ☐

Grammar 2: Conditionals (2) ▶ *CB page 88*

About the language

Third conditional

Form

If + past perfect + *would have* + past participle in the main clause

Use

To describe something in the past that could have happened, but didn't or something that shouldn't have happened, but did.

If you'd come to my party, you'd have met my new boyfriend.

If they hadn't taken the koala to the Wildlife Rescue Centre, she wouldn't have survived.

Typical mistakes

                                 had
If you ~~would have~~ been here earlier, you would have seen Maria.

                          wouldn't have got
If I had been wearing cream, I ~~hadn't got~~ sunburnt.

---

1   Match these sentence halves.

0	If I had caught the bus, …	a	I would have called you.
1	If I had eaten those mushrooms, …	b	I wouldn't have missed the concert.
2	If I hadn't lost my phone, …	c	I wouldn't have believed it was possible.
3	If I had won the competition, …	d	I wouldn't have had nightmares last night.
4	If I hadn't seen it myself, …	e	I would have spent the money on a new car.
5	If I hadn't watched that film, …	f	I would have been very ill.

0 _b_   1 ......   2 ......   3 ......   4 ......   5 ......

2   Complete these third conditional sentences with the correct form of the verbs in brackets.

0   If I _hadn't felt_ sick, I _wouldn't have been_ at home when the doorbell rang. (not feel, not be)

1   If I .... the door, I .... Bill. (not answer, not meet)

2   I .... to Australia if we .... going out together. (go back, not start)

3   I probably .... Damian if I .... Bill. (marry, not marry)

4   If I .... Damian, we .... at least four children. (marry, have)

5   If they .... girls, I .... them Delia, Samantha, Lily and Agnes. (be, call)

6   I .... Damian choose the names if they .... boys. (let, be)

7   Life .... very different if I .... the door that day. (be, not answer)

3   Combine these sentences to make third conditional sentences with *if*.

0   You didn't wait for the sales. You paid £100 for that jacket.

   If you had waited for the sales, you wouldn't have paid £100 for that jacket.

1   I got up late. I wasn't able to go to basketball training.

   ....

2   She didn't look at the weather forecast. She didn't know it was going to rain all day.

   ....

3   He stayed up late. He was tired in the exam.

   ....

4   He promised to change. I decided to come back.

   ....

5   I didn't listen to my friend's advice. I bought a big dog.

   ....

6   You didn't run as fast as I did last time. You didn't win the race.

   ....

4   Complete the second sentence so that it is similar in meaning to the first sentence, using the words given.

0   I don't like computers, so I still use a typewriter.

   If I _liked computers, I wouldn't still use a typewriter._

1   We visit my aunt on Saturdays when we're not too busy.

   If we ....

2   I forgot my keys last night. I broke a window to get in.

   If I ....

3   Jade's tennis will improve, but she has to practise.

   If Jade ....

4   Shona will catch the train, but she has to hurry.

   If Shona ....

5   I eat chocolate when I'm depressed.

   If I ....

6   Billy doesn't have a bicycle, so he walks to school.

   If Billy ....

Vocabulary 1: Numbers and measurements ▶ *CB page 83*

1   Match the figures in column A with the descriptions in column B.

Column A	Column B
0 50 kph	a) a period of time
1 37%	b) a distance
2 22 kilos	c) a year
3 16–18 hours	d) a weight
4 1939	e) a height
5 32	f) a percentage
6 over 100 kilometres	g) an ordinary number
7 7 centimetres tall	h) a speed

0 ..*h*..   1 ....   2 ....   3 ....   4 ....   5 ....
6 ....   7 ....

2   Complete these 'cat facts' with one of the figures from column A in Exercise 1.

Cat Facts

- Cats can run for short distances at speeds of up to (0) *50 kph.*

- They can, however, travel very long distances at a slower speed. There are many stories of cats taken from their homes who managed to find their way back. To do this they will walk (1) ....

- Cats have (2) .... muscles in each ear and can turn their heads up to 180° in both directions.

- Indoor domestic cats spend (3) .... a day sleeping, though they hardly ever sleep right through the night.

3   Look at these answers and complete the questions. Use the expressions in the box.

> how much you weighed   how far   how long
> what's the fastest speed   what percentage
> what's the population   ~~what year~~

A: (0) .... ***What year*** .... were you both born in?

B: I was born in 1989 and Tina was born in 1991.

A: (1) .... can you hold your breath for?

B: About half a minute but I'm sure I could hold it for longer under water.

A: (2) .... your class are female?

B: 95%. Diego is the only boy.

A: (3) .... do you usually like to sleep at night?

B: At least seven hours.

A: Do you know (4) .... when you were born?

B: Nearly six kilos!

A: (5) .... you've ever travelled at?

B: About 300 miles an hour on a plane.

A: (6) .... of your country?

B: I'm not sure but I think it's about 35 million.

A: (7) .... is your school from where you live?

B: Well, it's about seven kilometres.

- This relaxed lifestyle means that indoor cats generally live between 12 and 15 years. The oldest cat on record was called Puss. She died in (4) .... just one day before her 36th birthday.

- The heaviest cat was a male called Himmy. He weighed (5) ....

- The smallest, also a male, was called Tinker Toy. He was only (6) ....

- (7) .... of homes in the United States have cats and 35% of these households have more than one. This adds up to a total cat population of about 68 million!

Vocabulary 2: Story-telling devices ▶ *CB page 83*

1   Match the underlined story-telling devices to their uses.

1 <u>Honestly</u>, I didn't know what to say.

2 <u>Suddenly</u> everything was completely quiet again.

3 <u>Anyway</u>, we all decided it would be better to get a dog.

4 <u>Can you believe it?</u> Martina told Sandro about the surprise party.

5 <u>In the end</u> it wasn't such a difficult test and we all passed.

6 <u>You know</u>, I had never realised how kind she was.

a) to change the subject you are talking about

b) to emphasise that you are telling the truth

c) to show that something happened quickly

d) to show that you are about to finish your story

e) to give yourself time to think of what to say next

f) to emphasise how surprising something is

1 ......   2 ......   3 ......   4 ......   5 ......   6 ......

2   <u>Underline</u> the best alternative to fill in the gaps in this text.

I had the funniest experience with my neighbour's parrot, Toto. He's a big red and green bird and, though Tina is always telling me how sweet he is, I have always had my doubts. (1) *Honestly/Suddenly*, he really is very big and bad-tempered and we're all a bit afraid of him.

(2) *Anyway/Honestly*, one night I woke up in the middle of the night feeling very thirsty. I went into the kitchen to get a glass of water. I was half asleep and I didn't bother to turn on the light or anything. (3) *In the end/You know*, I didn't notice anything strange at all until I turned on the tap. It all seemed perfectly normal. (4) *Honestly/Suddenly* there was this terrible screech and something enormous and red and green flew past me.

(5) *Can you believe it?/In the end*, it was Toto the parrot. He'd somehow got in through my kitchen window and was sitting in the sink. He likes watching the water from the tap, apparently.
(6) *Anyway/Suddenly*, he was absolutely terrified and I didn't know how to calm him down. (7) *In the end/Suddenly* I had to phone Tina and ask her to come upstairs and get him.

Listening

1   🎧 Listen to different people telling stories about pets. Match the pets in the box to the speakers. (There are more pets than speakers.)

| fish   rabbits   bird   dog   mice |
| hamsters   tortoise |

Speaker 1 ....

Speaker 2 ....

Speaker 3 ....

Speaker 4 ....

2   🎧 Listen again and decide whether the statements are true (T) or false (F).

Speaker 1

1 She took Lucky home because she had always wanted a pet. ☐

2 She now realises why Lucky was abandoned. ☐

3 She felt very sorry for Lucky. ☐

Speaker 2

4 He decided to get Jimmie so that Freddie wouldn't be lonely. ☐

5 He thinks that Freddie and Jimmie don't like each other. ☐

Speaker 3

6 She always found it difficult to get Tweety back into his cage. ☐

7 She was worried because she couldn't find him. ☐

Speaker 4

8 He thought that it was a long walk to his friend's house. ☐

9 He was shocked to see that Harry could jump so high. ☐

10 He was relieved that Bill couldn't jump over the fence. ☐

Speaking: Coming to a decision

1 Put this conversation into the correct order.

a) **Karina:** Yes, that's a good idea. I agree. We don't really know what kind of music he likes, so let's get the book.

b) **Nicholas:** Mmm that's a good suggestion, but we don't really know what kind of music he listens to.

c) **Karina:** So, what are we going to give Sebastian for his birthday?

d) **Diego:** OK, well what about a book? I saw a fantastic book on endangered animals the other day. We could give him that.

e) **Diego:** Well, why don't we buy him a CD? He really likes music.

f) **Kasia:** No, and I haven't ever seen him listening to his personal stereo or anything.

0 ..*c*.. 1 .... 2 .... 3 ....

4 .... 5 ....

2 Look at the conversation between Davinia, Stelios and Ela and match the <u>underlined</u> parts to the functions in this list. The first one has been done for you as an example.

a) make a suggestion ...2..
b) agree with a criticism ......
c) ask for suggestions ......
d) say you agree with an idea ......
e) criticise a suggestion ......
f) make another suggestion ......
g) give the reason for the decision ......
h) make the final decision ......

Davinia: So, [1]<u>what are we going to do</u> this weekend?

Stelios: Well, [2]<u>why don't we</u> go for a walk in the mountains? We haven't done that for a long time.

Davinia: Mmm [3]<u>that's a good suggestion, but</u> it might not be warm enough.

Ela: [4]<u>No, and</u> they said on the weather forecast that there might be thunderstorms.

Stelios: OK, well [5]<u>what about</u> inviting some friends around for supper? We haven't seen Lucas and Patricia for ages. We could invite them.

Davinia: [6]<u>Yes, that's a good idea. I agree.</u> [7]<u>We don't really know what the weather is going to be like,</u> [8]<u>so let's invite some people round here.</u>

3 Write this conversation using the prompts and the ideas in brackets.

0 **Dan:** (*ask for suggestions*) So, pet/get?
So, what kind of pet are we going to get?

1 **Tim:** (*make a suggestion*) Dog? Fun to play with.
....

2 **Anna:** (*reject suggestion*) Too difficult to look after in flat.
....

3 **Lauren:** (*agree with rejection*) Difficult to train.
....

4 **Tim:** (*make an alternative suggestion*) Cat. Very clean and don't have to take for walks.
....

5 **Dan:** (*express agreement with the idea; state reason for decision; state final decision*)
....
....
....

Writing: Report ▶ *Writing Reference page 157*

1 Look at these two reports and the advice on writing reports. Which report follows the advice?

⚡ **Writing reports**
DO use headings
DO use formal language.
DO state facts
DON'T give personal opinions till the conclusion

Report A

Here are some things you should think about if you're going to buy a pet. Let's start with dogs. They're OK. I mean, they're friendly and fun to play with but who's going to take a dog for a walk a couple of times a day? Not me, that's for sure. The dog will get very bored and fat. He will bark a lot. The neighbours will complain. What about cats? Great, but they don't like being moved. If you go on holiday you can't take them with you. You have to get a friend to come and give them their food. What about birds? I think they're a fantastic idea because they don't cost very much and you can move them easily. They make really good pets. You know, I think birds are the best choice.

Report B

Introduction
The main aim of this report is to discuss briefly the good and bad points of having exotic pets.

Present situation
Exotic animals are fascinating, so people think they will be good pets. The problem is that we do not know very much about how to look after animals like these and give them the wrong food. Consequently, they get ill and sometimes even die. Another problem is that the animals are sometimes brought here illegally so if we buy them, we help the people who break the law by taking them from their natural environment.

Conclusion and recommendation
It is very good for people to be interested in animals. However, if they want to learn more about exotic animals, they should visit zoos and wildlife reserves. Animals like cats and dogs are better pets.

2 Find and underline examples of informal language in Report A.

3 Find and underline three 'linkers of consequence' in Report B.

⚡ **Linkers of consequence**
We use linkers of consequence to connect a cause and a consequence. The following are common linkers of consequence.

cause	linker	consequence
We didn't have very much space	**so**	*we had to choose a small pet.*
Our dog barked all the time.	**Consequently,**	*our neighbours were not very happy.*

4 Rewrite the first report in your notebook so that it follows the advice for report writing.

11 Danger!

Grammar 1: Making comparisons ▶ *CB page 91*

About the language

Making comparisons

Lions **>** *monkeys*
  dangerous
*Lions are **more dangerous than** monkeys.*

Alligators **=** *lions*
    dangerous
*Alligators are **as dangerous as** lions.*

Dolphins **<** *alligators*
    dangerous
*Dolphins are **less dangerous than** alligators.*

one-syllable adjectives:	clean fast tall	cleaner faster taller	(the) cleanest (the) fastest (the) tallest
one-syllable adjectives ending in -e:	large brave	larger braver	(the) largest (the) bravest
one-syllable adjectives ending in a vowel + a consonant:	big fat	bigger fatter	(the) biggest (the) fattest
adjectives ending in -y:	dry dirty	drier dirtier	(the) driest (the) dirtiest
two-syllable adjectives ending in -le, -er, -ow:	simple clever narrow	simpler cleverer narrower	(the) simplest (the) cleverest (the) narrowest
other two-syllable and three- or more-syllable adjectives	honest beautiful	more honest more beautiful	(the) most honest (the) most beautiful
irregular forms	good bad far	better worse further	best worst furthest

Typical mistakes

My sister's flat is ~~more~~ bigger than mine.
                        as
It isn't as expensive ~~than~~ my flat.

1 Compare Tim's car and Tina's car. Write three different comparative sentences for each adjective.

0 (big) *Tim's car is bigger than Tina's. Tina's car isn't as big as Tim's. Tina's car is less big than Tim's.*

1 (new) ....

....

2 (comfortable) ....

....

3 (fast) ....

....

4 (noisy) ....

....

5 (expensive) ....

....

2 Find four spelling mistakes in this text and correct them.

Lorne is one of the best beach resorts in Australia. It's very popular, but much quieter than Bondi beach. I love to surf there. My surfboard is biger and longer than my friend's board, but it's made of thiner fibreglass. It's also older. The new boards are made with lighter materials. They're a bit shorter and widder as well. They're also a lot cheaper than my board was!

3 Complete these sentences with the comparative or superlative forms of the adjectives in brackets.

0 I find swimming .... *easier* .... than running. (easy)

1 But I find surfing .... than snowboarding. (difficult)

2 I also think it's .... than any other sport I know. (exciting)

3 In fact I would say that surfing is one of the .... experiences you can have. (enjoyable)

4 I think I am .... on a surfboard than I am at any other time. (happy)

5 Of course, when there are no waves there's nothing .... than sitting on your board waiting, especially if it's cold. (boring)

4 Use one word only to fill in each gap in this text.

Your own home is one of the (0) ....*most*.... dangerous places to be in. Experts say that (1) .... accidents occur at home than anywhere else. The kitchen is the (2) .... room in the house for accidents. You are (3) .... likely to injure yourself there than you are driving a car or playing sport. However, it is easier to prevent accidents (4) .... most of us think. For example, avoid leaving pans of oil to heat up while you do something else. Fires can start easily. Water and other liquids are (5) .... dangerous than oil or fat, but they can cause serious burns too. The second (6) .... important cause of injuries at home is falling. A lot of people are (7) .... careful than they should be when they climb a ladder or get up on a chair to change a light bulb. It's always better to be safe (8) .... sorry. Always check that the ladder or chair is on a flat surface.

Grammar 2: Giving advice ▶ *CB page 94*

About the language

Giving advice

We use *should* and *why don't you* to give advice.
We can also use *ought to* but it is less common.

*You look very tired. You **should go** to bed early tonight.*
***Why don't you** go to the doctor?*
*You **ought to invite** Maria to the party.*

We can use *should* in the negative. We don't usually use *ought to* in the negative.
*You **shouldn't eat** so much – it's not good for you.*

We can also use *should* and *ought to* to talk about obligations and duties.

*You **should** tell Dan if you know where his keys are.*
*You **ought to** phone your mother more often.*

1   Write sentences giving advice. Use the verbs in the box and *should, why don't you* or *ought to*.

go   ~~tell~~   ask   buy   borrow

0 A: I'm always late for my first class at college.
   B: You ....***ought to tell***....... the teacher to wait until you get there. (ought to)

1 A: The trouble is it takes about an hour on the bus.
   B: .... by car? (Why don't you)

2 A: But I don't have a car.
   B: Well, ... your father to buy you one. (should)

3 A: He wouldn't do that.
   B: Then .... one yourself? (Why don't you...?)

4 A: But I don't have any money.
   B: .... some from the bank. (should)

Typical mistakes

You should ~~to~~ buy a new car.
Why you (don't) learn to swim?

2   Complete these comments a third person made about the advice in exercise 1.

0 You ....***shouldn't tell***.... the teacher to wait for you. You .....***should get up***..... a bit earlier.

1 You .... by car. You .... by bicycle.

2 You .... your father. You .... your mother instead.

3 You .... a car, you .... a lift with a friend.

4 You .... from the bank. You .... a job and save up.

3   Complete these sentences so that they mean the same as the sentence given.

0 I think it would be a good idea to have a picnic on Sunday.
   Why........***don't we have***........ a picnic on Sunday?

1 I think you should buy some new trainers before you go on holiday.
   I think .... to buy some new trainers before you go on holiday.

2 It would be better to get a ladder than to stand on that chair.
   You .... a ladder instead of standing on that chair.

3 It's dangerous to leave hot oil on the cooker.
   You .... hot oil on the cooker.

4 I suggest you try to drink more water.
   Why .... to drink more water?

4   Look at this advice for students who are having problems with their English. There are some mistakes with *why don't you*, *should*, *shouldn't* and *ought to*. Find the mistakes and correct them.

1   I think you should to buy a computer and use the Internet. You can download songs and even movies and read about all your favourite celebrities.

2   Why you don't ask the teacher to let you work with another group if you don't think the members of your group get on well together?

3   You should to not feel shy. Your classmates probably find English pronunciation just as hard as you do.

4   There are lots of good English–English dictionaries and some have great pictures. You ought go to a bookshop and look at them.

5   In my opinion, you shouldn't to worry about understanding every word. I'm sure you wouldn't understand every single word if you listened to the news in your own language!

5   Now match the advice to these problems.

a)
> Whenever our teacher says we are going to listen to a recording, I get really nervous. There are always so many words that I don't understand.

b)
> I don't find the reading and listening exercises in my book very interesting.

c)
> The group of people I work with in class don't get on well together. Whenever the teacher asks us to discuss something, there is a terrible silence.

d)
> I have a bilingual dictionary but I think I should have an English–English dictionary as well. Can you recommend a good one?

e)
> We often have discussions with the whole class, but I feel really shy about my pronunciation. Even though I often have an opinion I don't want to say anything in case my classmates laugh at me.

1 ......   2 ......   3 ......   4 ......   5 ......

Vocabulary 1: Describing jobs/qualities needed for jobs ▶ *CB page 92*

1   Look at these pictures of different jobs and match them to the words.

cartoonist ..*0*.. , waiter .... , private detective ...... , window cleaner ...... , swimming instructor ......

0

1

2

3

4

2   Look at the text below and <u>underline</u> the best alternative.

A ....

It's not very (1) *well paid/badly paid* but I make a lot of money from tips. Some of the customers are not very polite, though and that makes the job very (2) *exciting/stressful*. I have to take the orders, bring the meals and then add up the bills. If you make a mistake, people can get very angry so you need to be (3) *good with numbers/imaginative*.

B ....

In my job you need to be good at drawing but it's also important to (4) *have a good sense of humour/be brave*. You need to be very (5) *imaginative/patient* to think up a new idea every day.

C ....

Well, you need to be a bit
(6) *imaginative/curious* because you have to
be interested in other people. The job can
sometimes be (7) *dangerous/boring* because
people get very angry if they find out you
have been following them. So people like me
are usually quite (8) *brave/good with
numbers*.

D ....

You have to have (9) *a good head for
heights/a good sense of humour* and be quite
(10) *patient/fit* because we climb up and
down ladders all day. The job isn't as
(11) *dangerous/well-paid* as everyone thinks
but you do have to be careful where you put
your feet.

E ....

Anyone who teaches anything has to
be (12) *good with numbers/good with people*,
but if you teach a sport to young children
you also need to be very (13) *curious/patient*.
They get upset very easily, especially if things
don't go well.

3   Read the texts again and write the
job at the top of each text.

Vocabulary 2: Survival
▶ *CB page 95*

1   Find ten words for the items on the
right in this wordsearch grid.

B	L	A	N	K	E	T	M
A	T	S	P	A	D	E	A
N	O	P	H	M	A	L	T
D	R	I	O	C	O	P	C
A	C	R	N	K	E	T	H
G	H	I	E	R	O	P	E
E	T	N	P	M	A	C	S
H	E	R	W	A	T	E	R
M	I	R	R	O	R	I	N

2   🔊 Listen to two students discussing this task and
complete their conversation.

> Below are some things you might want to take on a
> camping trip in the mountains in case of an emergency.
> Decide between you which five items are most
> important.

Lucy: Well, I think we should definitely take
         (1) .... It's very easy to get
         dehydrated, even in the mountains.

Luke: Yes, but not if there's snow or ice. I think the bandage
         (2) .... It would be useful
         for stopping the bleeding if one of us had a cut and
         we could also use it for other injuries.

Lucy: OK. I agree. What about the torch?

Luke: The batteries might run out, so I think we ought
         to take the mirror as well. We can use it
         (3) ....

Lucy: Yes, that's a good idea. I don't think the phone is very
         important, do you?

Luke: No, not in the mountains, it wouldn't work, but I do
         think (4) .... the thermal
         blanket.

Lucy: Yes, if we have to spend a night in the open, it could be
         very important. But we could take the matches too so
         that we can (5) ....

Luke: Mmm. The trouble is matches get wet. We can always
         use the mirror to light a fire.

Lucy: Yes, that's true. We can only have one more thing,
         so (6) .... spade? We could
         dig a hole in the snow if we need to, and
         (7) .... from the cold.

Luke: OK. So, we'll take: the bandage, the torch, the mirror,
         the thermal blanket and the spade.

Reading

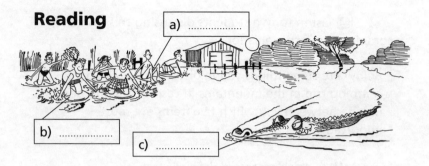

a) ....

b) ....

c) ....

1 You are going to read an article about a brave teenager. Before you read, label these things in the picture.

> boogie board   the shore   an alligator

2 Read the text and answer this question.

Does Amanda Valance think she is braver than other people? ......

Brave beyond her years

Fourteen-year-old Amanda Valance had no idea that she would have to save her best friend's life on a warm summer's evening in 2001.

The moon shone on Little Lake Conway in Orlando, Florida as Amanda and her friend Edna Wilks, also fourteen, floated on their boogie boards. With four teenage boys, they went out to about 40 metres from the shore. Edna was <u>drifting</u> with her arms in the warm water when suddenly she felt something pulling her arm. 'One of the boys must be playing a trick on me,' Edna thought.

She looked into the water and screamed in terror. A four-metre alligator was staring back at her with its jaws around her arm. She thought, 'This is how I'm going to die.' A few seconds later the alligator had pulled her under the water.

When Edna had screamed everyone else had swum <u>frantically</u> to the shore. Everyone, that is, except Amanda. 'I heard Edna scream,' she says, 'and it was really awful. It was like a scream of death.' She knew that Edna was in danger and she couldn't leave her best friend to die.

As she looked out over the dark waters for Edna, the alligator came up for air. Amanda heard her friend's screams again. Edna used her right arm to try and get her left arm free of the alligator's jaws. It finally moved away for a moment and Amanda immediately swam over to help her.

'There was blood everywhere and her left arm was badly <u>mangled</u>,' Amanda says. 'We could see the alligator swimming around. I was so scared he was going to attack both of us, but I knew I had to get Edna to shore.'

Amanda handed her boogie board to Edna. She swam beside her friend and pushed her while she looked for the alligator. Edna was <u>panicking</u> but Amanda tried to stay calm. 'I just kept telling Edna that I wouldn't leave her and that we were going to be OK.'

The others had called an ambulance and it arrived just after the girls reached the shore. Edna spent a week in hospital and she is still <u>recovering</u> from her injuries.

Since the terrifying incident, the girls have become even closer than they were before. 'While I was in the hospital,' Edna says, 'I told Amanda how much I love her. If she hadn't come back for me, I have no doubt that I would have died. She saved my life.'

Even now Amanda doesn't think of herself as a hero. 'I'm just glad I was able to help,' she says simply.

3 Before you read the text again, choose the correct alternative to answer these questions. Circle your answer.

1 What did Edna think when she felt something pulling on her left arm?
   A That Amanda was playing a game.
   B That she was being attacked by an alligator.
   C That the boys were playing a game.
   D That she must play a trick on the boys.

2 How did the boys react when they heard Edna scream?
   A They went to help her.
   B They called to Amanda.
   C They tried to get away.
   D They stayed in the water.

3 Where was Edna when Amanda started looking for her?
   A Under the water with the alligator.
   B On her boogie board.
   C Swimming towards the shore.
   D Swimming towards Amanda.

4 What does Edna think would have happened if Amanda hadn't helped her?
   A She would have been killed.
   B The alligator would have let her go.
   C They wouldn't have been friends.
   D She wouldn't have been in hospital.

4 Match the <u>underlined</u> words from the text to these dictionary definitions.

a) feeling so frightened that you cannot think ....

b) moving along slowly in the air or water ....

c) becoming healthy again after being ill or injured ....

d) badly damaged by crushing or twisting ....

e) hurriedly and in a way that is not organised ....

Writing: Informal letters ▶ *Writing Reference pages 149 and 151*

1 Look at the sentences below. They are from two different letters. Decide if the sentences are formal or informal. Mark them I or F.

1 I would be very grateful if you would send me some information about degree courses in aeronautical engineering. ☐

2 I was teaching my class when I looked round and noticed that one of the kids wasn't there. ☐

3 How are you? I'm fine but I've been really busy lately. ☐

4 I would like to thank you in advance for your help. ☐

5 Luckily, it turned out she had just gone back to the changing rooms to get her swimming cap. ☐

6 Although I do not plan to work during my stay, I would also like to receive information about visa requirements. ☐

7 I've been earning a bit of money teaching swimming at the local pool. ☐

8 Last week something really terrifying happened. ☐

9 I recently completed my secondary education here in Italy. ☐

10 I look forward to receiving the information and visiting your country in the near future. ☐

11 It really gave me a fright because, for one terrible moment, I thought that she might have drowned. ☐

12 Write soon and let me know what's happening in your life. ☐

13 I am writing to enquire about the possibility of studying in Australia. ☐

2 Now look at the sentences again and put them in order to make two letters: a formal letter and an informal letter.

Formal letter: ....

Informal letter: ....

3 Look at this task and the letter a student wrote. There are too many details and the letter is too long. Cut the unnecessary details.

Write a letter to a friend telling them about a dangerous incident. Your letter should be between 120 and 180 words long.

Dear Magda,

It was really great to get your letter. ~~It arrived yesterday morning at 11.30 a.m.~~ It's always good to hear all your news.

I wanted to tell you about something really terrifying that happened to a friend of mine a couple of weeks ago. His name is James and I met him last summer when we were on holiday in Sardinia. Anyway, he was on his new purple and yellow, fibreglass surfboard at a beach near here when suddenly he saw a grey, black and white shark with big sharp, white teeth swimming towards him. He was really terrified but luckily, he had read an article about sharks in a magazine called 'Surf the Globe' the day before. The article, which was written by someone called Lana Beachworth, said that the best thing to do if a shark swims towards you is to hit it. Unfortunately, my friend didn't have anything to hit the shark with so he had to use his hand. Can you believe it? He punched the shark on the nose. In the end, it swam away and my friend was able to paddle back to shore. This took him about five minutes. He was shaking when he came out of the clear blue water.

Well, that's my main piece of news. Apart from going to the beach, I'm studying a lot for my exams in mathematics, chemistry, geography and English and looking forward to coming home for the holidays. Will you be around in August? Write and let me know.

Love,

Marta

Do you remember?

Grammar 1: *can/could/be able to*
▶ *CB page 99*

About the language

Can/could/be able to

Use

can

We use *can* to talk about present and future ability.

He **can play** the violin.
They **can't start** the work until next month.

could

We use *could* to talk about general past ability.

She **could walk** before she was a year old.
Could you speak French when you were ten?

We also use *can* and *could* in requests

Can you carry the shopping for me?
Could you lend me your bicycle?

be able

We use *am/are/is able to* to talk about present ability.

He **is able to swim** 500 metres in ten minutes.

We use *will be able to* to talk about future ability.

We**'ll be able to move** house next spring.

We use *was/were able to* to say that somebody managed to do something on one occasion (usually something that was not easy).

He **was able to hold** his breath for five minutes.

! Typical mistakes ....

We spent all day walking around and finally we
were able to find
~~could find~~ *a cheap hotel.*

1 Five of these sentences have mistakes. Find and correct the mistakes and then tick (✓) the other sentences.

1 My mother could to speak Chinese when she was young.

2 Were you able go to the bank at lunchtime?

3 I don't be able to see you today.

4 Can you finish the report by Friday?

5 I couldn't get tickets for the concert.

6 We don't can afford to buy a new car.

7 Will you be able to come to the party?

8 Can you be able to help me with this exercise?

2 Write questions with *be able to* about these comments. Use the verbs in the box.

| borrow | drive | afford | get | ~~come~~ |

0 A: I'm having my 18th birthday party next Monday night and I'm inviting all my friends.

 B: __*Will*__ they __*be able to come*__ on a Monday night?

1 A: I'm going to go out and buy a Ferrari the next day.

 B: .... you ....
such an expensive car?

2 A: I'll get the bank to lend me the money.

 B: .... you .... so much?

3 A: And I want the Ferrari to be pink with blue spots.

 B: .... you .... one like that here?

4 A: I haven't passed my driving test yet.

 B: .... you .... it if you haven't got a licence?

3   Decide whether you can use *could* and *was/were able to* in these sentences. If you can only use *was able to*, cross out *could*. If you can use both, put a tick (✓).

0   I *was able to/could* get to the bank just before it closed.   ☐

1   He *was able to/could* speak several languages by the time he was twelve.   ☐

2   They *were able to/could* get tickets for the concert on Friday.   ☐

3   She *was able to/could* find out how to pronounce *memorise* by looking it up in a dictionary.   ☐

4   We *were able to/could* meet our friends for a coffee on the last day of our holiday.   ☐

5   You *were able to/could* read at least a year before you started school.   ☐

4   Choose the correct word for each space. Circle your answer.

My cousin Lucy has a photographic memory. If she reads a page in a book, she (1) ……………… remember the whole thing word for word. She (2) ……………… study nearly as hard as me. I revised every day for a week before our last history test and I still (3) ……………… remember a lot of important dates. Luckily, I (4) ……………… remember a lot of other information and I always get extra marks for that. Lucy only read through the chapters we had studied once the night before and she (5) ……………… get all the questions right. I (6) ……………… get her to tell me how she does it.

1   **A** could   **B** must   **C** can

2   **A** doesn't have to   **B** mustn't   **C** couldn't

3   **A** didn't have to   **B** couldn't   **C** mustn't

4   **A** can   **B** had to   **C** was able to

5   **A** was able to   **B** could   **C** can

6   **A** must   **B** have to   **C** can

Grammar 2: *used to* ▶ *CB page 102*

About the language

used to

Form

Positive statements:	*used to* + infinitive
Negative statements:	*didn't use to* + infinitive
Questions:	*did you/she/they* etc. + *use to* + infinitive

Use

We use *used to* to talk about past habits and states that do not occur now or no longer exist.

We **used to own** *a boat, but we sold it last year.*
I **didn't use to like** *fish, but now I love it.*
She **used to drive** *to work, but now she cycles.*

❗ Typical mistakes ·················

used
I ~~use~~ to go to the swimming pool every day in summer.

used
I ~~use~~ to sing in a band but I don't any more.

use
Did you ~~used~~ to spend your summer holidays in the mountains?

use
I didn't ~~used~~ to like olives but I do now.

play
I used to ~~playing~~ tennis a couple of times a week, but I hurt my arm and had to stop.

1 Put the words in order to make sentences with *used to*.

0 in summer your family did go away use on holiday together to?
Did your family use to go away on holiday together in summer?

1 Yes. coast on used two weeks to we always go to a guesthouse the for.

....

2 use did go to time same always you at the?

....

3 Yes same used see the people to we always and

....

4 what your holiday most did you use enjoy to about?

....

5 food was only thing use <u>didn't</u> to enjoy we the the

....

2 Use the prompts to write sentences with *used to*.

0 I / live / London.
I used to live in London.

1 Tina / be / my closest friend.

....

2 We / meet up / every day

....

3 We / go / café / have coffee and talk.

....

4 Tina / tell / very funny stories.

....

5 She / work / a big department store.

....

6 Princess Diana / be / a customer there.

....

7 She / wear / beautiful clothes.

....

3 Write five sentences with *used to* about these two pictures. Use the prompts.

In the nineteenth century …

00	*Most people used to wear hats.*	(hats)
0	*People didn't use to drive cars.*	(cars)
1	....	(horses)
2	....	(electric lighting)
3	....	(mobile phones)
4	....	(long dresses)
5	....	(jeans)

Vocabulary 1: Memory ▶ *CB page 100*

1   <u>Underline</u> the best alternative to fill in the gaps in this story.

I've got a really terrible (0) *memory/memorise* for faces. Last week I was walking along my street when a girl came up to me and said 'Hi Max. How are you?'. The trouble was, I couldn't (1) *remember/remind* ever having seen her before in my life.

'You've (2) *forgotten/memorised* who I am, haven't you?' she said.

'No, of course not,' I answered. 'It's just that my mind's gone blank for a moment. (3) *Remind/Remember* me. When was the last time we saw each other?'

'It was that (4) *unforgettable/forgetful* night in June when Felix had his 18th birthday party,' said the mystery girl. 'You (5) *remembered/memorised* my phone number and promised to ring me the following week.'

'Look, I've got a piece of paper with me now so why don't you give me your name and number again. I won't (6) *forget/leave* to phone you this time,' I said.

'Why don't you tie a knot in your handkerchief as a (7) *memory/reminder?*' said the girl, whose name was Marta. 'Many (8) *forgetful/forgettable* people do that.'

Anyway, a week later when I was doing my washing I saw the knot in my handkerchief. Can you believe it? I couldn't (9) *remember/memorise* what it was for. Luckily Marta didn't (10) *forget/remember* to phone me.

2   Use the word given in capitals at the end of each line to form a word that fits in the space.

1   If you study chemistry, you have to .... a lot of formulae. MEMORY

2   My friend Simon is one of the most .... people I know. FORGET

3   He wrote her name on his hand as a .... to phone her later. REMIND

4   Sailing across the Atlantic Ocean was a truly .... experience. FORGET

3   Match the first parts of the sentences in Column A to the second parts in Column B.

Column A

1   He lost …

2   I forgot …

3   Remember …

4   The smell of fresh apples always brings back memories …

5   I left …

6   I've got a good memory …

7   Remind …

Column B

a) of my childhood.

b) to tell Anna that she has a dentist's appointment this afternoon.

c) for faces but I can't remember names.

d) all about my friend's birthday.

e) me to go to the post office later.

f) my camera on the train.

g) his memory after hitting his head in the accident.

1 ......   2 ......   3 ......   4 ......   5 ......

6 ......   7 ......

Vocabulary 2: Prefixes
▶ CB page 103

1   Match the prefixes on the left to the words on the right. You need to use some of the prefixes twice

a) ir   1 possible

b) un   2 legible

c) dis   3 friendly

d) il   4 patient

e) im   5 visible

f) in   6 responsible

                 7 honest

                 8 comfortable

2   Fill in the gaps in these dictionary definitions with a word from Exercise 1.

1 If something is ...., it cannot happen or you cannot do it:

   It was .... to get tickets for the game.

2 Someone who is .... becomes angry because they have to wait:

   Don't be so ....! It's your turn next.

3 If something is ...., you cannot see it:

   Germs are .... to humans.

4 If you feel ...., you do not feel physically relaxed:

   She felt really .... because the man was standing so close to her.

5 Likely to steal, lie or cheat:

   A .... businessman.

6 Behaving in a careless way without thinking about the bad results you might cause:

   It's .... to leave small children alone.

7 Difficult or impossible to read:

   Her writing is ....

8 Not behaving pleasantly; unkind:

   Some of the kids in my class are really .... towards me.

Reading

1   Read the article below once quickly and tick (✓) the best title.

   A Macy: a case of missing identity

   B Macy: the woman who forgets everything

It's as if Macy's life began two weeks ago. She found herself alone and <u>shivering</u> from the cold on the side of a completely unfamiliar road.

She remembers feeling a <u>bump</u> on the back of her head and looking in the pockets of her jeans and long <u>brown coat</u>. She found $24.31 and a pink cigarette lighter. (That was all) she found. (1) ....*e*........... .

It was just after midnight on March 2nd when she went into a phone box outside a petrol station near a small town in Virginia, USA and (dialled the emergency number 911.) (2) ....*d*........... . She can't <u>recall</u> how long she walked that night and she can't remember anything else.

Macy has a classic case of amnesia. (3) .... She has no memories of friends or family and no memories of playing with classmates as a child. She doesn't know if she is a wife or a mother or if she has a favourite colour. She doesn't remember any films, books, names, faces or places. She didn't recognise the President of the United States when she saw him on television or remember any recent events.

Medical experts say cases like Macy's, in which there is such a complete loss of memory, are quite <u>rare</u>. (4) .... Usually the effects do not last long and the period of time that the person has forgotten is normally limited.

Macy's doctors said medical tests show that she is healthy. They think something really terrible might have happened to her and that this has made her mind cut off all her memories. (5) ....

Macy has noticed some things that seem familiar. A <u>desire</u> to paint her nails pink made her think she might have enjoyed doing that before. (6) .... She can't explain why she chose the name Macy, but wonders if it has something to do with her past.

Macy's doctors say all she can do is wait. She says she is also praying, although she doesn't even know if she has ever done that before.

2   Read the complete article again. Choose the most suitable sentence from the list a–f below for each gap 1–6 in the article. Circle the words or phrases that helped you decide. Two have been done for you already.

a) Macy says she wants to know about her past even if it is very frightening.

b) Walking around a lake made her feel that she had always liked being outside in the fresh air.

c) This illness can be caused by a head injury to the brain or by a shocking event.

d) She told the operator she didn't know where she was – or who she was.

e) There was no wallet and nothing to identify her.

f) Everything before March 2 is completely blank.

3   Match these dictionary definitions to the underlined words in the text.

a) a small raised area on the surface   ....

b) a strong feeling that you want something very much   ....

c) shaking because you are cold   ....

d) remember   ....

e) unusual   ....

Listening

1   You will hear four people talking about things they forgot. Look at the subjects A–E and the words and expressions 1–10. Which words and expressions are connected to each of the subjects?

1   answered some really easy questions

2   so small

3   you're gorgeous

4   from my best friend, Julia

5   little Michael

6   entered a competition

7   special occasion

8   inside a book

9   red rose

10   wedding anniversary

A an important celebration   *7, 10*   ....

B a lucky win   ....

C an important letter   ....

D a romantic gesture   ....

E a new baby brother   ....

2   Now listen to the recording. For each person, choose which of the subjects in the list (A–E) they are talking about. Write your answers below. There is one extra subject which you do not need to use.

Speaker 1   ☐
Speaker 2   ☐
Speaker 3   ☐
Speaker 4   ☐

3   Each of the people forgot something about the event. Match the things they forgot (A–E) to the speakers. Write your answers below. There is one extra thing which you do not need to use.

A something she had been reminded about

B a rule

C the questions

D what she was wearing

E a person's appearance

Speaker 1   ☐
Speaker 2   ☐
Speaker 3   ☐
Speaker 4   ☐

4   Now listen again to check your answers.

Speaking: Describing a photograph

1 📼 Look at the task below and listen to the student describe one of the photographs. Tick (✓) the photograph that the speaker describes.

> **Please compare and contrast these photographs and say which one looks more enjoyable to you.**

2 📼 Listen again and fill in the gaps in these sentences from the description.

1 It .... the beach – I'm ....

2 It's .... a hot day because they're all wearing summer clothes.

3 It .... a father, a mother and two children.

4 Everyone .... and looking very happy.

5 I think .... this kind of picnic.

3 Complete this description of the other photograph. Use the words in the box.

covered	sea	on	better	prefer	outside

The second photograph shows a different family eating (1) .... This might be their garden – I can see some flowers and the back of a house. They are sitting (2) .... chairs and there is a table (3) .... with food. There are six people in this family, an older man, probably a grandfather, and some younger people. Everyone is smiling and happy again. The food looks much (4) .... in this picture, but think I would (5) .... to be at the beach, because I love the (6) ....!

Writing: Story ▶ *Writing Reference page 155*

1 Look at this task and the story a student wrote. For each of the gaps two of the alternatives are possible and the other alternative is not. Put a tick (✓) next to the possible alternatives.

Write a story about a time you forgot something very important.

> I had never bought a lottery ticket before. My friend Patrice bought one too. I put mine safely in the pocket of my jeans.
>
> I had a very bussy week that week. (0) .... we had friends staying with us but I was helping prepare for Elise's surprise birthday party as well. (1) .... by Saturday night I had completely forgoten about the lottery ticket.
>
> I sat down to watch TV. (2) .... Patrice phoned me to say that we had won. The trouble was I couldn't remember where had I put the ticket. (3) .... I remembered where it was and then I had a terible thought. What if Mum would have already washed the jeans?
>
> I was rushing out to the laundry. (4) .... I found my jeans and there in the pocket was the wining ticket!

0	A To begin with ✓	B Firstly ✓	C Eventually
1	A At that moment,	B So,	C As a result,
2	A Just then	B Eventually	C At that moment
3	A In the end	B At the end	C Finally
4	A Eventually	B Finally	C As a result

2 There are four spelling mistakes and three grammar mistakes in the letter. Find them and correct them.

UNIT
13 Down under

Grammar 1: *like* ▶ *CB page 110*

About the language

like

like as a verb
like + *-ing* (= enjoy doing)
*I **like** cooking because I also **like** eating!*

would like **+ (object) + infinitive with** *to*
a polite way of saying 'want'. It refers to the future.
*I'**d like to** take you to the cinema.*
Would you like to *borrow my dictionary?*

like as a preposition
When we use *like* as a preposition, it means 'similar to' or 'in the same way as'.

*He really **looks like** his father.*
*Listen! It **sounds like** someone is calling for help.*

> **Typical mistakes**
> going
> *I like g̶o̶ to the cinema on Saturday afternoons.*
> ● *He looks l̶i̶k̶e̶ angry.*

---

1 Use these prompts to write sentences about Paula.

| 0 | dance | ✓ | get up early | ✗ |

Paula likes dancing but she doesn't like getting up early.

| 1 | cook | ✓ | wash up | ✗ |

| 2 | surf | ✓ | ski | ✗ |

| 3 | swim | ✓ | mountain bike | ✗ |

| 4 | visit museums | ✓ | visit art galleries | ✗ |

| 5 | watch horror films | ✓ | watch romantic films | ✗ |

2 Underline the best alternative to complete these sentences.

0 I *like/would like* to go somewhere different on holiday this year.

1 My friend Johannes *likes/would like* going to unusual places.

2 He asked me if I *would like/liked* to go with him to an island called Formentera.

3 Johannes *wouldn't like/doesn't like* staying in hotels.

4 This year he *would like/likes* to rent a house or an apartment.

5 I *would like/like* to find a place with a swimming pool.

6 He *wouldn't like/doesn't like* swimming, but he *would like/likes* to find a house near the beach as he really *would like/likes* looking at the sea.

3   Complete the second sentence using *would like* so that it is similar in meaning to the first sentence.

0   Do you want to go to Australia?
    Would you like to go to Australia?

1   Yes, but I want to see New Zealand too.

    ....

2   My friend wants to study in Australia.

    ....

3   Do her parents want her to do that too?

    ....

4   No, they don't want her to be so far from home.

    ....

5   They want her to study in Europe.

    ....

4   There are mistakes in some of these sentences. Find the mistakes and correct them. Put a tick (✓) next to the sentences without mistakes.

0   Do you like outdoor activities? ✓

1   I like to visit Tasmania at the end of my trip to Australia.

2   I like travelling with my friend Eva. We get along really well.

3   We'd like some information on the north coast of Tasmania.

4   Do you like information on driving or coach tours?

5   I'd like you to come with me when I go to the travel agents.

6   I'd like looking at travel magazines and dreaming about my next holiday.

5   Complete these sentences with *like* and one of the verbs in the box.

sound	~~look~~	smell	sound	taste	look

0   I .... *look like* .... my sister. We've both got fair hair and blue eyes.

1   We .... anyone else in our family, though. They're all dark with brown eyes.

2   These crisps really .... pizza!

3   Your suntan lotion .... fresh coconut.

4   I don't know who the singer is but he .... Ricky Martin.

5   That .... your sister's car. It makes a terrible noise!

Grammar 2: *so/neither/nor* ▶ *CB page 115*

About the language

so/neither/nor

	swimming	tennis	football	horse-riding	running	chess
Maria	✓	✓	✗	✗	✗	✓
Ricky	✓	✓	✗	✗	✓	✗

AGREEING

so

Maria **likes** swimming. **So does** Ricky.
Maria **went** swimming yesterday. **So did** Ricky.
Maria **can** play tennis well. **So can** Ricky.

neither/nor

Maria **doesn't like** football. **Neither/Nor does** Ricky.
Maria **won't watch** the football tomorrow. **Neither/Nor will** Ricky.
Maria **can't ride** a horse. **Neither/Nor can** Ricky.

DISAGREEING

Ricky **likes** running. Maria **doesn't**.
Ricky **can't play** chess. Maria **can**.

Typical mistakes

I've seen all the Star Wars movies. So Francesca ~~has~~.

I didn't see 'Big Brother' on TV last night but Simone *did* ~~saw~~.

---

1 Complete these sentences.

0 I want to go to Canada. So __*does*__ my friend Eva.

1 She likes a lot of Canadian singers and so .... I.

2 She can speak French. So .... her brother Gaston.

3 We would like to find out about studying there and so .... Gaston.

4 Eva has saved a lot of money for the trip and so .... I.

5 Eva and Gaston bought their tickets yesterday and so .... I.

2 Complete these sentences agreeing with the negative statements.

0 **Ana:** I don't know much about Japan.
   Paula: Nor __*do*__ I.

1 **Ana:** I can't speak French.
   Paula: Neither .... I.

2 **Ana:** I haven't read any books about Italy.
   Paula: Nor .... I.

3 **Ana:** I won't visit Greece this year on holiday.
   Paula: Neither .... I.

4 **Ana:** In fact, I'm not really interested in travelling this year.
   Paula: Nor .... I.

3   Complete these sentences.

0 My friend Gemma really likes Enrique Iglesias, but I **don't**.

1 She says she'd like to go and live in Miami, but I ....

2 She's going to start learning Spanish, but I ....

3 She's got a boyfriend, but I ....

4 I'm going to Paula's party on Saturday night, but Gemma ....

5 Gemma went to Spain on holiday last year but I ....

6 She can't play the piano but I ....

7 She doesn't really like classical music but I ....

8 Gemma didn't watch the film on TV last night but I ....

4   The responses here are all incorrect. Write correct responses.

0 A: I don't speak German
    I do.
  B: ~~I speak~~.

1 A: I can't write it either.
  B: I write.

2 A: I won't go on the school trip to Germany.
  B: I go.

3 A: Paula doesn't like Gemma.
  B: I like.

4 A: I didn't see her last film either.
  B: I saw.

5 A: I'm not going to go out tonight.
  B: I'm going.

Vocabulary 1: The physical world
▶ CB page 109

1   Use the words in the box to complete these quiz questions and answers.

> desert   forest   mountain   river   lake   oceans
> island   lakes   continent

1 *Question:* In which .... would you expect to find the Kalahari ....?
  Answer: Africa.

2 *Question:* Australia is surrounded by the waters of two .... What are their names?
  Answer: The Indian and the Pacific.

3 *Question:* The Black .... is in which European country?
  Answer: Germany.

4 *Question:* On which .... in the Canaries is Spain's highest ....; what is it called and how high is it?
  Answer: Tenerife. It's called Mount Teide and it's nearly 4000 metres high.

5 *Question:* The city of Chicago in the United States is built on .... Michigan. What are the other famous North American .... called?
  Answer: Ontario, Huron, Superior and Erie.

6 *Question:* What is the longest .... in the world?
  Answer: The Nile.

2   Make words from the jumbled letters and match them to the icons.

1 o n a c l o v   ......
2 e l a k   ......
3 r e t a w l l a f   ......
4 d o w o   ......
5 c h e a b   ......
6 f l i c f   ......

3   Use the words from exercise 2 to complete this text.

There are lots of things to do on the island of Frivola. If it's hot and sunny, you will probably want to spend your time on one of the white, sandy (1) .... In the evenings you can walk along the (2) .... and watch the sunset. On cooler days, why not take the cable-car to the top of Mount Macondo? This extinct (3) .... is over 3000 metres high. As you walk down the mountain path you will pass through the fields where local farmers grow crops like bananas and papayas. Just outside the village, there is a magnificent (4) .... which provides water for the crops. It also fills the stunning (5) .... You can hire a boat or swim there. A walk in the (6) .... is also very enjoyable. Breathe the fresh mountain air and the scent of pine trees.

Vocabulary 2: Tourism ▶ *CB page 111*

1   Complete this crossword with words connected with tourism.

Across
1   full of people
3   all the entertainment that is available in the evening in a town
5   a journey in a plane
8   something you keep to help you remember a place

Down
2   shops in an airport that sell tax-free goods
4   a book that has information and advice about a subject
6   the railway system that runs under the city of London
7   the roll of thin plastic that you use in a camera to take photographs

2   Use the words from the crossword to complete this conversation.

Tamara: Guess what? None of my holiday photos came out. I didn't put the (1) .... in the camera properly.

Gaston: Hadn't you used it before?

Tamara: No. I bought it at the (2) .... shop just before we got on the (3) .... to London.

Gaston: You must have had a great time, though. What did you see?

Tamara: Oh, all the usual tourist attractions, but the best thing was the bus tour. Our (4) .... recommended taking an open-top bus trip round the city of London, and that was wonderful.

Gaston: Did you mainly use buses or the (5) .... when you were there?

Tamara: Buses, especially when we went out late to clubs. The (6) .... in London is fantastic, and lots of people then took night buses home. In fact, even late at night, the buses were always really (7) ....

Gaston: Did you buy any (8) ....?

Tamara: Yes, I got a really great poster with a photo of London taken from the air.

Listening

1 📟 You are going to hear a recorded Internet message about Queenstown in New Zealand. The first time you listen, tick (✓) things that are mentioned on the recording.

a  ☐   d  ☐

b  ☐   e  ☐

c  ☐   f  ☐

2 📟 Listen again and look at these notes a student made. Some information is missing. For each question, fill in the information in the numbered space.

3 Read the information below about Queenstown. Some of the information is different from the information on the recording and some is the same. Mark the answers D (different), or S (same).

1 Queenstown was the first place in New Zealand to have bungy jumping. ☐

2 You can't see the lake from the gondola ride. ☐

3 People of all ages will enjoy the boat trip. ☐

4 You can only take the boat trip on the lake in the morning. ☐

5 A lot of the buildings in Arrowtown are over a hundred years old. ☐

6 You can't go skiing at night anywhere else in New Zealand. ☐

Queenstown, New Zealand

Bungee jumping
Single jump: $159
All three jumps together: (1) ....

Gondola Ride
Trip only: (2) ....
With lunch included: $44

TSS Earnslaw: (3) .... -year-old steamboat
Trip takes (4) ....

Arrowtown
(5) .... from Queenstown
Lake District Museum open from 10 to 5
Closed (6) .... afternoon

Coronet Peak
Skiing and snowboarding all levels
Night skiing every day from (7) ....

Writing: Article ▶ *Writing Reference page 158*

1   A student has written an article about the most interesting city she has ever visited, but the paragraphs are in the wrong order. Put them in the right order.

a   Of course I'm describing Hong Kong. I had wanted to visit it ever since I was a child because my father went there and brought back lots of fascinating souvenirs.

b   Back in Hong Kong, why not get the Peak Tram and look out from the top over the lights of the city. The view is truly unforgetable.

c   After all that shopping, take a ferry over to the island of Lamma. You can walk from the pretty little port to some lovely sandy beaches. Stop for diner in one of the seafood restaurants before you get the ferry back to Central.

d   Obviously the first thing that everyone thinks of when you mention Hong Kong is shopping and it really is a shopper's paradise. You can get everything there from the lattest electronic equippment to silks and fine teas.

e   The most interesting city I have ever visitted has fantastic modern architecture, wonderful shopping and natural beauty only twenty minutes from the centre.

1 ......   2 ......   3 ......   4 ......   5 ......

2   Look at these two plans. Which one is the plan the student wrote?

A

Para 1:   What Hong Kong has: architecture, shopping, nature

Para 2:   Why Hong Kong: father went/brought back souvenirs

Para 3:   Shopping: ('shopper's paradise')

Para 4:   Nature: Lamma Island ('pretty little port')

Para 5:   Views: City lights from Peak Tram ('truly unforgettable')

3   Look at these comments from the student's teacher. Which comments were written about:

A   the article in exercise 1?   ☐

B   another article the student wrote a few weeks ago?   ☐

1

You've got some good ideas, but there are some problems here. First of all, the article isn't divided into proper paragraphs and you haven't used some of the interesting vocabulary we looked at in class. Next time try to make a very complete plan before you write your composition. Make a note of the interesting vocabulary you want to use. And don't forget to check your work for spelling and grammar mistakes.

2

This is very good. You've used quite a lot of interesting vocabulary and you have divided your article up into paragraphs very well. I think this was because you wrote such a good plan first. I was very pleased to see that you had taken my advice about making a note of any interesting vocabulary that you want to use. There are some spelling mistakes, though. Don't forget to check your writing.

4   Find and correct the six spelling mistakes in the article from exercise 1.

B

Para 1:   Introduction

Para 2:   The city I have chosen

Paras 3 and 4:   What you can do there

Para 5:   Conclusion

UNIT 14 Elements of nature

Grammar 1: Countable and uncountable nouns ▶ CB page 119

About the language

Countable and uncountable nouns

	Countable nouns	Uncountable nouns
singular	My car is in the garage.	Traffic in London is terrible.
plural	I have three cats.	–
a/an	She's got a coat, an umbrella and some boots.	–
some and any	We've got some tomatoes but we haven't got any bananas. Have you got any oranges?	We've got some rice, but we haven't got any bread. Have you got any cheese?

The following are common nouns that are **usually** uncountable:
accommodation, advice, bread, English (and all other languages), *fruit, furniture, information, luggage, rice* (and all other grains and cereals), *spaghetti, traffic, travel, water* (and all other liquids).

The following are common nouns that can be countable and uncountable:
chocolate, coffee, chicken, glass, hair, iron.

> ### Typical mistakes
>
> *are*
> The people here ~~is~~ usually very friendly.
> *some* *s*
> I bought ~~a~~ new trouser⌃

1 Underline the best alternative to complete this text.

I'd really like to buy (0) a/_some_ new furniture for our flat. The furniture we've got at the moment (1) *look/looks* terrible and we haven't got (2) *much/many* anyway. Some of the chairs (3) *is/are* badly worn and the table (4) *is/are* badly scratched. It's also got (5) *a/some* mark on it from where Tina put (6) *a/some* hot frying pan on it.

The bedroom (7) *isn't/aren't* much better and the kitchen (8) *is/are* a disaster. We haven't got (9) *many/much* cupboards so we have to put things on top of the bench. The rice (10) *is/are* in a jar there and so (11) *is/are* the spaghetti. There's also usually (12) *some/a* bread, (13) *some/a* fruit in a bowl and a bottle of olive oil, which (14) *is/are* very good here.

People who (15) *come/comes* to the flat always (16) *say/says* how nice it looks but I don't agree. It's very difficult to find (17) *a good/good* accommodation here and this flat was the best thing we could get. Before we came to live here we got (18) *an/some* information from the embassy and we asked our friends to give us their (19) *advice/advices*. One thing they didn't warn us about was the (20) *traffic/traffics*, which (21) *is/are* very noisy.

They didn't warn us about the traffic!

2 Complete these sentences with *a*, *an* or no article.

0 Would you like ......*a*...... chocolate? I think there are one or two left in the box.

1 Do you have .... iron? I'd like to press these trousers.

2 Are we having .... chicken for dinner again?

3 I forgot to get .... coffee when I went to the supermarket. Can you get some when you go out?

4 She's got .... lovely curly dark hair.

5 One of my friends had .... pet chicken when he was a child.

6 How much is .... small black coffee?

7 Could I get you .... glass of water?

8 You've got .... chocolate all over your t-shirt.

9 She makes very attractive ornaments from .... coloured glass.

10 We cook most of our meals in a heavy pot made of .... iron.

Grammar 2: Articles ▶ *CB page 124*

About the language

Articles

We use the indefinite article, *a/an*:
- for single countable nouns mentioned for the first time
- for jobs

*There's **a big tree** at the end of the garden.*
*He's **an engineer**.*

We use the definite article, *the*:
- for previously mentioned nouns
- when there's only one of something

*There's a big tree at the end of the garden. Let's sit under **the tree** to have our picnic.*
*It's very cloudy tonight – I can't see **the moon**.*

We use no article:
- for most streets/towns/cities/countries/names
- for uncountable, plural and abstract nouns

*She's lived in **Australia** for ten years.*
*We need **bread**, **cheese** and **wine**.*

1 Complete these sentences. Use the pictures to help you.

0 Once upon a time there was ....*a beautiful*.... ....*princess*.... who lived in ....*a castle*....

1 She had almost everything she wanted apart from one thing. She did not have ....

2 Sometimes she also thought it would be quite nice to meet ....

3 One day the princess decided to go for ....

4 While she was walking, she met ....

5 He said if she gave him .... he would grant her one wish.

6 She kissed him and .... appeared.

7 'Oh no,' said the princess. 'I really wanted ....'

2   Use these prompts to write sentences about the princess and prince in exercise 2.

0   prince / not know / what do.
   The prince didn't know what to do.
   ....

1   tried / comfort / princess.
   ....

2   started / walking back / castle / together.
   ....

3   on / path / saw / frog.
   ....

4   'Look / there's / frog!' said / princess.
   ....

5   'You granted / wrong wish!' said / princess / to frog.
   ....

6   'Where's / bicycle / I wished for?' said / princess.
   ....

7   'you want / bicycle / or / prince?' asked frog.
   ....

8   'I want / keep / prince / have / bicycle / as well!' said princess.
   ....

3   There are mistakes in some of these sentences. Put a tick (✓) next to the sentences that are correct and change the sentences with mistakes.

0   I went to ~~the~~ London last month.

1   Tania came with me.

2   She's from the Peru.

3   She plays tennis really well.

4   We did a lot of shopping in the Oxford Street.

5   We bought a lot of souvenirs and presents.

6   I got my brother a huge block of the chocolate.

Vocabulary 1: The weather ▶ *CB page 121*

1   Choose the best alternative to complete this conversation. Circle your answer.

Angelo: What was the weather like when you were in Australia?

Maria: Well, when we got to Perth it was really (1) .... and (2) ....

Angelo: What was the temperature?

Maria: In the high thirties. It was a real shock because when I left London, it was absolutely (3) .... The maximum that day was only 4° C.

Angelo: And was the weather good the whole time you were in Australia?

Maria: Yes, it was really. In Adelaide it was a bit (4) .... than it had been in Perth but there were still (5) .... skies. Melbourne was nice too except that it was very (6) .... The only places we had (7) .... were Hobart and Brisbane.

Angelo: Isn't Brisbane in the north?

Maria: Yes and it's very tropical. There was this incredible (8) .... while we were there. It was really exciting.

1   A hot   B mild

2   A cloudy   B sunny

3   A boiling   B freezing

4   A milder   B warmer

5   A cloudy   B clear

6   A sunny   B windy

7   A rain   B snow

8   A thunderstorm   B wind

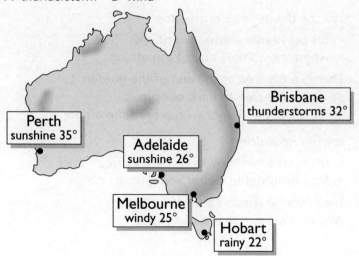

Perth
sunshine 35°

Adelaide
sunshine 26°

Brisbane
thunderstorms 32°

Melbourne
windy 25°

Hobart
rainy 22°

Vocabulary 2: Phrasal verbs with *take*

▶ *CB page 119*

1 Match the phrasal verbs to the nouns.

1 take in   a) work or responsibility

2 take up   b) a person you have just met

3 take to   c) an older relative

4 take off   d) a company or a job

5 take over   e) some complicated or surprising news

6 take after   f) a sport or hobby

7 take back   g) time (a few minutes, a week, a year etc.) from work or study

8 take on   h) something you have said

2 Replace the verbs in italics in this story with phrasal verbs with *take*. Write your answers below.

I really (0) *liked* Carmen when she first came to work in the hotel. I had known her older sister, Julia for years and Carmen (1) *behaves and looks like* her in lots of ways. After Julia left to go to London, Carmen (2) *got control of and responsibility for* her job. We were working together until the end of July when I was (3) *having* a few days' holiday. The week before, the boss asked us if we would be willing to (4) *accept* some extra work. I explained that I was going to be very busy after I came back from my holiday because I had decided to (5) *start going* swimming in the evenings. He got very angry and said that if I wouldn't do the extra work I could start looking for another job. Carmen just smiled and said she would be happy to do the work. It was so incredible I really couldn't (6) *understand it completely*. Julia was a really wonderful person and I thought Carmen was like her. I was completely wrong.

0 *took to* ....

1 ....

2 ....

3 .... a few days ....

4 ....

5 ....

6 ....

Speaking

1 🖭 Look at these pictures and the questions above them and then listen to the discussion that two pairs of students had. In which discussion do the students ask for each other's opinion? ......

> 1 Which of these campaigns have you had in your city, town or region?
>
> 2 Which ones do you think would work best where you live?

HELP CLEAN UP THE COAST
Come along on Saturday

NO MORE PLASTIC BAGS!
Take a basket

MY TOWN WITHOUT MY CAR
Leave your car at home on Wednesday 17th September

Sort out your rubbish!

2 Phrases a–k are from the first discussion you heard in exercise 1. Match each phrase to one of the following categories 1–5.

1 Giving your opinion

2 Agreeing

3 Disagreeing

4 Pausing to think about your opinion

5 Asking someone for his/her opinion

a) In my opinion, making people leave their cars at home is a really good idea. ......

b) That's right. ......

c) We had that day in my town too. A lot of people complained about it, but I think it was a success. ......

d) Do you think that would work where you live? ......

e) No, not really. ......

f) Do you agree? ......

g) I'm not sure. ......

h) Sometimes I think many people are just selfish. ......

i) Well, it depends. ......

j) What do you think? ......

k) I don't agree at all! ......

Reading

1 Read the article on page 101 about astrology once through quickly and match these pictures to the numbered paragraphs.

a) ......   b) ......

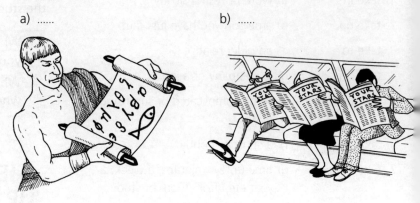

2 Look at the list of headings below. Now read the article more carefully and choose the most suitable heading (A–F) for each paragraph. <u>Underline</u> parts of the text which tell you the answer. One heading is not needed.

A Some ups and downs

B Origins

C Of course I don't really think it's true

D A good businessman

E A lucky astrologer

F Should we trust the stars?

3 Use words from the text to complete these sentences.

1 There is a lot of scientific .... that smoking is bad for your health.

2 It was my .... to meet someone like Marcelo that year.

3 My brother loves astronomy, so my parents bought him a .... last Christmas.

4 Last year, I .... to a great new magazine called 'Super Science'.

5 I .... that I occasionally read my horoscope, but I don't take it seriously.

c ......

d

e

Written in the stars?

0 _Should we trust the stars?_ ....

If you look at almost any newspaper, you'll find a horoscope in it. But <u>is there any scientific evidence</u> for thinking that the positions of the planets influence our behaviour, destiny or personalities? For most scientists the answer is 'Definitely not!'

1 ....

It was the ancient Greeks who made astrology popular. Every Greek was given a horoscope, so astrologers had to invent more sophisticated methods to make the horoscopes different from one another. By the 1st century BC, astrology had become the complicated system we know today.

2 ....

Astrology went in and out of fashion until the telescope was invented in the 17th century. Once people could actually see the planets they stopped believing in astrology. By the 18th and 19th centuries almost nobody was making horoscopes anymore.

3 ....

But in 1890 a salesman named William Allan offered people who subscribed to his astrology magazine a free horoscope. This was such a success that by 1903 he was employing nine people to make up horoscopes and send them out to paying customers.

4 ....

Today only a few people admit to taking astrology seriously though many more read their horoscopes in newspapers and magazines. Whether they believe what they read or not is another question.

Writing: Transactional letter ▶ _Writing Reference page 149_

1 Look at these two plans and the transactional letter. Which plan matches the letter the student wrote? ......

Plan A

Paragraph 1:   Introduction - things to do this weekend

Paragraph 2:   Saturday morning shopping - _The Lanes_

Paragraph 3:   Saturday afternoon - Sunny? Palace Pier

Paragraph 4:   Bad weather? Brighton Pavilion

Plan B

Paragraph 1:   Introduction – thanks for letter

Paragraph 2:   Description of souvenir shops in Brighton

Paragraph 3:   Description of a palace in Brighton

Paragraph 4:   Plans for Friday

Dear Jamie

Thank you for your letter. I'm really pleased you're coming to Brighton. I've planned some things for us to do.

First of all, I think you would enjoy doing some shopping in 'The Lanes'. There are a lot of fascinating shops where you can buy presents and (a) <u>souvenirs</u> of Brighton. (b) <u>However</u>, they can be quite expensive!

Another good place for (c) <u>souvenirs</u> is the Palace Pier. I thought it would be nice to walk along the promenade and go to the pier in the afternoon. (d) <u>If it's a sunny day</u>, it's a lovely walk.

(e) <u>If it turns out to be cold and wet</u>, I thought we could go to the Brighton Pavilion. (f) <u>It's</u> a museum that used to be a palace right in the centre of town.

See you on Friday.

Best wishes,

Nourredine

⚡ **Linking sentences in a paragraph**

We link sentences in a paragraph by

- using reference words:

  I met <u>Nourredine</u> in Algeciras. <u>He</u> was waiting for the bus and I asked him what the time was. It was the first time I had been <u>there</u>.

- parallel expressions (= different words for the same or a similar thing):

  People first walked on the moon in <u>1969</u>. That was <u>the same year</u> The Beatles broke up.

  I didn't sleep at all that <u>night</u>. The next <u>morning</u> I was exhausted.

- linking words and expressions (e.g. *then, however, in addition*):

  I like most sports. I'm not very good at them, <u>however</u>.

- using the same words from one paragraph in the next.

  I think it was the best <u>concert</u> I've ever been to.

  Another great <u>concert</u> was REM at Wembley last year.

2   Look at the <u>underlined</u> words and expressions in the letter on page 101 and match them to the things in this list.

1 using reference words   ......

2 parallel expressions   ....

3 linking expressions   ......

4 using the same words from one paragraph
   in the next   ....

3   Look at this letter a student wrote. Some linking words are missing. Use the linkers from the box to complete the letter. Write your answers in the spaces provided in the letter.

> as well   in the afternoon   first of all

4   The ideas in the paragraphs are also not linked properly. Replace the <u>underlined</u> words and phrases in the letter with the expressions in the box. Write your answers on the lines below.

> I'd like   ones   there   it's raining
> get something

1 ....

2 ....

3 ....

4 ....

5 ....

Dear Nourredine,

It was really good to get your letter. It sounds like Brighton is fun. I'm looking forward to coming to see you (1) <u>in Brighton</u>. I think I might be able to come the week after next. Here are the things I'd like to do.

(a) .... I'd like to go shopping on Saturday morning. I hear the shops are very interesting and I want to buy some presents for my family.

(b) .... I would like to see the beach and the area along the seafront. I hear there are a lot of art and craft stalls along the seafront. (2) <u>I want</u> to (3) <u>buy a present</u> for my friends (c) .... We could go to the Pier if the weather is fine.

If (4) <u>the weather is not fine</u>, we could go to a museum. Are there any other interesting (5) <u>museums</u> in Brighton apart from the Pavilion?

See you the week after next.

All the best,

Fatima

UNIT

15 The business of food

Grammar 1: Passives (past and present) ▶ *CB page 127*

About the language

Passives (past and present)

	Active	Passive
Present simple	*Many people speak English all over the world.*	*English is spoken all over the world.*
Present continuous	*They're building a new shopping centre in town.*	*A new shopping centre is being built in town.*
Past simple	*He sent the letter by express post.*	*The letter was sent by express post.*
Past continuous	*Someone was stealing the fruit from the trees.*	*The fruit was being stolen from the trees.*

Typical mistakes ....

      served
Lunch is ~~serving~~ between twelve thirty and three in the afternoon.

1 Make present simple passive sentences. Use the verbs in the box.

sell   ~~clean~~   serve   produce   perform

Hotel Windsor

0 All rooms ....*are cleaned*........... between 8 and 11 a.m.

1 The paintings in your room .... by local artists and may be purchased. Please contact the Desk Manager for details.

2 The hotel's famous cabaret show *The Windsor Experience* .... every Saturday night, in the Windsor Bar, from 9 p.m. until midnight.

3 Exotic food from all over the world .... in our gourmet restaurant, 'The Food Chain'.

4 Souvenirs, newspapers and magazines .... in our shop.

2   Write present continuous passive sentences about these situations. Use the words in brackets.

0   **Freddie:**   I think I'll go back to bed.

    Parker: I'm afraid your room _is being cleaned_ (clean), sir.

1   **F:**   Well, I'll go for a walk then. Where are my shoes?

    P: I'm afraid .... (polish), sir.

2   **F:**   And where's my favourite shirt? I want to get dressed.

    P: I'm afraid .... (iron), sir.

3   **F:**   Well, if I can't get dressed, I'll have some breakfast.

    P: I'm afraid .... (prepare), sir.

4   **F:**   I may as well have a game with Fido, then.

    P: I'm afraid .... (walk), sir.

3   Complete these comments Freddie makes about his house. Use the past simple passive of the verbs in the box.

> ~~build~~   sell   paint
> design   import

0   The house .... _was built_ .... in 1523.

1   It .... by a famous architect.

2   All the carpets .... from India.

3   A portrait of my great-great-grandfather .... by Rembrandt.

4   Unfortunately, quite a lot of the land .... when I ran out of money!

Grammar 2: Causative _have_ and _get_ ▶ CB page 129

About the language

Causative _have_ and _get_

Form
have + object + past participle
get + object + past participle

Note: _have_ is more commonly used in writing; _get_ is used more informally.

Use
We use _to have something done_ to say that someone else did something for us. It usually means that we have employed someone to do a job for us.

I **had my nails manicured** yesterday.
He**'s going to have his bike repaired** tomorrow.
Let**'s get the locks changed** before we go away.

It can also be used to talk about something, often unpleasant, that happened to someone.

Sara **had her bag snatched** yesterday.

> **Typical mistakes**
>
> We **had** (painted) our house.
>
>   _cleaned_
> He is having his jacket ~~clean~~.

1   Complete these sentences about the differences between Freddie and Parker.

0 Parker washes his own clothes. Freddie *has his clothes washed for him.*

1 Parker cooks his own breakfast. Freddie
.... for him.

2 Parker polishes his own shoes. Freddie
.... for him.

3 Parker services his own car. Freddie
.... for him.

4 Parker makes his own bed. Freddie
.... for him.

2   Freddie went camping on his own last week. Write sentences about what happened.

0 *He couldn't have his clothes washed. He had to wash them himself.*

1 ....

2 ....

3 ....

4 ....

3   Freddie is talking to a friend. Write the questions the friend asks him.

0 **Freddie:**   Do you like my new hairstyle?

   Gwendolyn: Yes, very much. Where *did you have it done*?
   ....

1 **Freddie:**   My car's running much better, isn't it?

   Gwendolyn: Yes. When ....
   ....?

2 **Freddie:**   I'm tired of going to get the newspaper every morning.

   Gwendolyn: Why ....
   ....?

3 **Freddie:**   I'm picking up my new suit tomorrow.

   Gwendolyn: Where ....
   ....?

4 **Freddie:**   My watch isn't working very well.

   Gwendolyn: Why ....
   ....?

4   These sentence transformations have mistakes. Correct the mistakes.

0 The hairdresser is cutting her hair tomorrow morning.
                 her hair cut
   She's having ~~cut her hair~~ tomorrow morning.

1 Someone is cleaning her windows.
   She's **having cleaned her windows.**

2 His wallet was stolen while he was on holiday.
   He **got his wallet stolen** while he was on holiday.

3 A technician is repairing my computer.
   I **am repairing my computer** at the moment.

4 It would be a good idea to get someone to paint the living room.
   Why **we don't** get the living room painted?

Vocabulary 1: Buying and selling
▶ *CB page 128*

Unjumble the words in the box and use them to complete this extract from a report.

tnsemrevdatsi	cudtrops	temkar	mopynac
soremuncs	cheserra	dranb	gool

Report

Introduction

The aim of this report is to explain how Banana Sports Shoes can improve sales over the next five years. Our team interviewed one hundred and twenty (1) .... (60 women and 60 men) to find out what they think about sports shoes in general and about our new (2) .... (sandals and boots) in particular.

Results of the survey

The (3) .... is expanding all the time. More and more people are buying sports shoes. However, if we want to take advantage of this, we will have to make some changes.

We suggest the following:

- Raise our prices. Our (4) .... shows that people think cheap shoes are not good quality.

- Change our image. Our (5) .... is really old-fashioned and that makes people think the (6) ...., *Banana Sports Shoes*, is old fashioned too. We suggest a picture of a banana instead of the initials BSS.

- Have more (7) .... on television, especially during sports programmes.

Conclusion

If these changes are made, we believe that the (8) .... will sell more shoes than it has in the last six months.

Vocabulary 2: Food ▶ *CB page 131*

1 A student has labelled these pictures but he has made some mistakes. Correct them.

a cooker

a vegetable

a desert

rare vegetables

2 <u>Underline</u> the correct alternative to complete this conversation.

Diana: We've just bought a new (1) *cook/cooker*. It's gas but it's got an electric oven.

Manfred: I don't use my oven much except for (2) *baking/roasting* bread.

Diana: Don't you ever cook things like (3) *roast/baked* beef?

Manfred: No, never. We're all (4) *vegetables/vegetarians* in my house.

Diana: But what about (5) *deserts/desserts*? Don't you ever make cakes or puddings?

Manfred: Not really. I don't like (6) *sweet/savoury* things very much.

Diana: How about things like pizza? You need a good oven to cook pizza.

Manfred: Pizza's terribly (7) *fattening/fatty*, you know.

Diana: But not as much as (8) *boiled/fried* foods like chips.

Manfred: No, I suppose not, but I try to eat as much (9) *raw/rare* food as possible.

Listening

1 🔲 Listen to the five short extracts and number the food and drink in the order you hear about them.

a

b

d

c

e

a) ....

b) ....

c) ....

d) ....

e) ....

2   Read the questions again and choose the best answer. Circle your answer.

1 What is the connection between the two speakers?

   A They are married.

   B The woman is the man's doctor.

   C They are friends.

2 What do the boys think of the food the English families give them?

   A They don't like it at all.

   B They like most things about it.

   C They don't have very strong opinions about it.

3 What change does the woman make to her order?

   A She doesn't want chips after all.

   B She doesn't want onion with her hamburger.

   C She wants a strawberry milkshake instead of a chocolate milkshake.

4 Who is the man talking to?

   A his daughter

   B his wife

   C people watching TV

5 How does the woman feel about what people have been doing?

   A pleased

   B angry

   C excited

3   🔲 Listen to the recording again and check your answers.

Speaking

1 Look at this speaking task and the conversation that two students had. Some phrases for pausing to think and giving your opinion have been removed. Put the phrases (a–f) into the numbered spaces below.

a) In my opinion …

b) Well, it depends …

c) I don't agree at all.

d) I think you're right

e) I'm sure you're right but …

f) I agree they're fattening up to a point …

> Your school is going to open a new snack bar. What kinds of things do you think should be sold there?

Evangelina: What do you think?

Thomas: I think it would be a really good idea to serve hot soup in the winter.

Evangelina: (1) ……. One problem is that there isn't anywhere to sit down and eat it.

Thomas: (2) ……. perhaps they could put in some tables and chairs. They should sell crisps, chocolate and cakes, though.

Evangelina: Don't you think they're all a bit fattening?

Thomas: (3) ……. but not if you don't eat them all the time.

Evangelina: Salads are a good idea, aren't they?

Thomas: (4) ……. Most people like salads. Oh, they'll have to sell chewing gum and cigarettes.

Evangelina: (5) ……. (6) ……. chewing gum is really disgusting and I don't think people should be encouraged to smoke either.

2 🖳 Listen to the conversation and check your answers.

Writing: Report ▶ *Writing Reference pages 151 and 157*

1   Look at this task and the report a student wrote. Has the student done everything she was asked to do?

> A new canteen is going to be built at your school. The director of the school has asked you to write a report on the things students disliked about the old canteen and what kinds of food they think should be served in the new one. You have also been asked to find out what students feel about the sale of chewing gum and cigarettes. Write a report of between 120 and 140 words.

Introduction

(0) <u>You wanted to know what students think about the food in the canteen.</u> (1) <u>This is what they had to say.</u>

Canteen Preferences

Most people said that the furniture in the old canteen is very unattractive.
They thought the food was (2) <u>more or less OK, though.</u>
The majority of students think healthy things like salads are very good. They also like pizza.
(3) <u>So,</u> these things should be put on the new canteen menu.
(4) <u>About the chewing gum,</u> some people think it's acceptable and other people (5) <u>say 'no'.</u>
(6) <u>With cigarettes,</u> <u>though,</u> <u>it was a big 'no thanks'.</u>

Conclusion

(7) <u>Anyway,</u> students want new furniture in the canteen and some different kinds of food.
(8) <u>I'm not sure about</u> the chewing gum but almost everyone was against cigarettes.

2   Read these two comments from a teacher on students' reports. Which comment is about the report above?

....

A
It's good to see that you've used the right layout for a report but you haven't covered some of the points in the task. There are also a few spelling and grammar mistakes. One very good thing about your report is that it is written in formal language.

B
You have covered all the main points in the task and your report is very accurate: there are no grammar or spelling errors here. You've also used the right layout for a report. There is one problem, however. Sometimes you have used very informal language that is not suitable for a report.

3   Match these formal phrases below to the numbered sections of the report that have a similar meaning.

0 ..*d*..   1 ....   2 ....   3 ....   4 ....
5 ....   6 ....   7 ....   8 ....

a) It is difficult to be certain about …

b) Here are the results of the survey I conducted.

c) To sum up, …

d) I was asked to do some research into students' attitudes to the canteen.

e) Regarding chewing gum …

f) All students, however, made it clear that they did not want cigarettes sold.

g) acceptable, however.

h) Therefore …

i) disagree

Unit 2 (p.15)

Vocabulary: Free time activities

ARE YOU A BORING 'COUCH POTATO'?

Key

If most of your answers were **A**'s, you are a bit of a couch potato. You need to do more interesting things in your free time.

If most of your answers were **B**'s, you are an interesting person with lots of different free time activities.

If most of your answers were **C**'s, you are a very active person with a lot of different interests. Perhaps you need to relax a bit more!

Answer key

UNIT 1

Grammar 1 p.5

1
1 Is he in our class?
2 Does he live near the school?
3 Has he got a sister called Claudia?
4 Does he play football for the school team?
5 Has he got a motorbike?
6 Are you meeting him after school today?

2 1 Where   2 How   3 What   4 How many   5 Who
6 Why/Where   7 What

3
1 How do you spell your name?
2 Where are you living at the moment?
3 What do you do?
4 How many brothers and sisters have you got?
5 How often do you go to the cinema?
6 When did you last go out with friends?
7 How long have you been learning English?
8 Why are you learning English?
9 How much does it cost to see a film in your city?
10 Which country would you most like to visit?
11 Who is one of your favourite singers?
12 Whose advice do you listen to most often?

4 b 1   c 11   d 2   e 4   f 6   g 10   h 8   i 9   j 7   k 3
l 12   m 5

5
1 What subject do you teach?
2 Where do you work?
3 Do you enjoy your job?
4 How many students do you have?
5 Are you married?
6 Who gets out of bed first in your house?

Grammar 2 p.7

1 1 A   2 A   3 B   4 B   5 A

2
1 Could you tell me when you started learning English?
2 I'd like to know if/whether you enjoyed your first
   English class.
3 Could you tell me what the name of your English
   book is?
4 I'd like to know if/whether you are coming to class
   tomorrow.
5 Could you tell me if/whether you like playing football?

3
1 how you spell your surname?
2 where you live?
3 if/whether you live alone.
4 how many of you live at that address?
5 if/whether you are studying or working.
6 how much you spend on entertainment each week?
7 what kinds of entertainment you enjoy most?

Reading p.8

1 1 C   2 E   3 B   4 A

2 1 ✓   2 ✗   3 ✓   4 ✗   5 ✓   6 ✗   7 ✗

Vocabulary p.9

1 1 Stefan   2 David   3 Rafaella   4 Claudia

2 1 B   2 A   3 A   4 B

3 & 4
1 part – noun – acting job
2 auditioned – verb – did an acting test
3 delighted – adjective – pleased
4 amazed – adjective – surprised
5 scrumptious – adjective – delicious
6 hectic – adjective – busy

Speaking p.10

1

	Mario	Donatella
family holidays	✓	✗
watching TV	✓	✗
family celebrations	✓	✓
shopping	✗	✓
going to museums and art galleries	✓	✓

2
1 Do you like
2 What about
3 What about
4 Do you like

3
1 really enjoy, like
2 don't really like
3 love
4 hate

Tapescript

D = Donatella   M = Mario

D: Do you like going on holiday with your family?
M: Well, in the summer we always go and stay with my
grandparents in the Pyrenees. I really enjoy that but I like
to go camping or to music festivals with friends too.
What about you?
D: I don't really like family holidays. Last year we went to
Corsica and we argued all the time. Where shall we eat,
when shall we eat, what beach shall we go to, when is
best to go to the beach, what shall we watch on TV… .
It was terrible!
M: That's funny. In my family we argue about the TV a lot.
Luckily I've got one in my bedroom so I can watch the
programmes I like best.
D: I don't like watching TV very much. I prefer listening to
music and I love playing it too. Every year on my father's

birthday we have a big family celebration and we all play something for him. It's great.

M: Yeah. I like family celebrations too, especially birthdays. But you usually have to go shopping for presents – that's the problem. I hate shopping. Especially with my sister Gloria. She's impossible.

D: I love shopping with my sister. She always has fantastic ideas for presents.

M: What about going to museums and art galleries? Do you like doing that kind of thing with your family?

D: Yes, I do. On Sundays we sometimes go to an exhibition after lunch. I really enjoy it.

M: Oh. We do that too. My brother's studying art and he always knows really interesting exhibitions. Last Sunday we went to see a new …

Writing p.11

1 1 lieing – lying
2 makeing – making
3 easyer – easier
4 matchs – matches
5 babys – babies
6 peace – piece
7 foreing – foreign
8 cuboard – cupboard

2 1 We've also got a lot of pets.
2 There are three goldfish, a canary, two cats and a dog.
3 The dog, who is called Jasper, is white with one black ear.
4 We've had him for about three years now.
5 After I finish my exams I'm going on a long holiday with my friends.
6 We're going to travel through Spain and stay at my uncle's house in Barcelona.

3 terrifyd – terrified
takeing – taking
makking – making

4 The Big Friendly Giant was very different to the other giants in Giant Land. He didn't eat children and all the other giants did. He wasn't nearly as big as the other giants either, they were all much taller and much uglier. However, the most important difference was that the Big Friendly Giant loved children. He wanted to save them from the bad giants. He and Sophie went to tell the Queen of England about the bad giants. Sophie and the Big Friendly Giant showed the Queen's soldiers the way to Giant Land. When they got there, they captured the bad giants and Sophie and the Big Friendly Giant lived happily ever after.

UNIT 2

Grammar 1 p.12

1 1 make T   2 boils T   3 keep F   4 enjoy F
5 speak F   6 causes T   7 makes F   8 eat T

2 1 She normally uses the exercise machines and she sometimes has a sauna afterwards.
2 This means she hardly ever gets home before ten o'clock.

3 On week nights, she doesn't usually go to bed any later than eleven o'clock.
4 Of course, at the weekend she doesn't ever go to bed that early.
5 She often goes out dancing and she sometimes dances all night!

3 1 Do I know you from somewhere?
2 I am studying at the same college as you.
3 Do you come here often?
4 I sometimes come here on Saturdays
5 I don't like the music very much.
6 Do you like it?
7 I prefer Latin music, actually.
8 Do you speak Spanish?
9 No, I don't speak it
10 I understand quite a lot.
11 What does 'Yo quiero bailar toda la noche' mean?
12 it means 'I want to dance all night!'

4 1 never gets home   2 is often   3 doesn't sleep
4 (usually) gets up   5 (always) has   6 (usually) goes
7 doesn't often   8 hardly ever sees

Grammar 2 p.14

1 1 am trying   2 doesn't seem   3 Do you know
4 think   5 Do you want   6 is talking
7 does it worry   8 go   9 always record   10 watch

2 1 Do you like   2 They are thinking of   3 She seems
4 Are you seeing   5 Do you see   6 I understand
7 I'm having   8 Are you doing, I've got

Vocabulary p.15

1 1 play   2 go   3 go to   4 play   5 take   6 collect
7 play   8 Going to, Playing

3 1 C   2 C   3 C   4 B   5 C   6 B   7 A   8 A

Learner training p.16

2 1 b   2 d   3 f   4 a   5 c   6 e

Listening p.17

1 The following sections are mentioned: 2 – Gorillas, 3 – Planet penguin, 6 – Cinema, 10 – Parrot show, 12 – Dolphinarium, 13 – Parrots

2 1 A   2 B   3 B   4 C   5 A   6 B

Tapescript

Welcome to Loro Parque, where you can experience many of the world's natural wonders: animals, tropical plants and exotic cultures. You can spend the whole day at the park, which is open from 10 o'clock in the morning to 8 in the evening. Why not leave your car and take our free train service from the centre of town? It only takes fifteen minutes. There's so much to see at Loro Parque and a day ticket, which gives you access to all the sections, is only 20 euros for adults and 10 for children. Start by visiting our specially designed cinema and seeing the film 'Nature Rediscovered', first shown in 1992 at the EXPO in Seville. Then start to explore. The parrot show, which gives the park its name, is held four times a day at 10.30, 1.30, 3.30 and the last show is at 5.30. Loro

Parque has the largest collection of parrots in the world. You will be amazed by their beauty and intelligence. Apart from these fantastic birds you can see many other animals. Our group of six male gorillas live in a specially built enclosure just like where gorillas live in the wild. If it's marine animals that interest you, then the Dolphinarium is the place to go. There are two dolphin shows a day: one at 12.00 and another at 4 in the afternoon. You'll love these friendly and intelligent creatures. You can also see the penguins in their specially created enclosure where snow falls and the water temperature is the same as the ocean around Antarctica. Why not stop for lunch at one of our three restaurants: enjoy pizza, grilled meats and fresh fish or stop for a coffee and a sandwich in the snack bar. Yes, there are wonderful things to see and do at Loro Parque. Come and experience it!

Writing p.18

1 1 B   2 A

2 1 A   2 B   3 B   4 C

UNIT 3

Grammar 1 p.19

1 1 Smoking   2 Taking/Bringing   3 Taking
4 Having/Leaving   5 Eating, drinking   6 Taking

2 1 Going for job interviews makes me feel anxious.
2 Getting up late makes me feel lazy.
3 Taking vitamin tablets makes me feel stronger.
4 Getting enough sleep makes me feel more relaxed.
5 Shouting loudly at other people makes me seem aggressive.
6 Eating a lot of fat and sugar makes me feel unhealthy.

3 1 b   2 d   3 e   4 c   5 a

4 1 Before   2 for   3 to   4 about   5 without   6 of
7 for   8 of   9 Without   10 before

Grammar 2 p.20

1 1 I really enjoy cooking.
3 I'm considering going to Paris to study at a famous cooking school.
4 I could only go if I manage to improve my French.
5 A friend suggested going to a language school.
8 I've agreed to teach them Italian in exchange.
10 We plan to spend half the time on French and the other half on Italian.
12 When I finish studying, I always cook myself a delicious meal.

2 1 to have   2 washing   3 to leave   4 to speak
5 helping   6 killing   7 spending   8 to visit   9 to drive
10 learning

Vocabulary p.21

1 1 information   2 impression   3 improvement
4 enjoyment   5 alteration   6 excitement
7 weakness   8 security   9 flexibility   10 laziness

2 1 security   2 alterations   3 improvement   4 Information
5 weakness   6 enjoyment   7 impression   8 excitement
9 Laziness   10 flexibility

3 -ment   -ion/-ation   -ness   -ity
improvement   information   weakness   security
enjoyment   impression   laziness   flexibility
excitement   alteration

Reading p.22

1 a 3   b 1   c 4   d 2   e -

2 1 Japan is noisier than other countries because, **as well as the usual city sounds, there are also thousands of recorded public announcements.**
2 (correct)
3 **You hear announcements telling you to be careful** when you are walking along the street.
4 (correct)
5 At the beach they **warn you that the sand is hot.**
6 **Some people really like the announcements.**

3 1 B   2 A   3 A   4 B   5 B   6 A   7 B   8 B   9 B

Speaking p.24

1 Photograph 2

2 1 look Swiss   2 look like   3 look as if   4 look as if 5 looks smart

3 1 looks as if   2 looks   3 looks like   4 looks as if
5 look like

Tapescript

The first one shows a restaurant or a café with people eating and drinking. I think it was taken in Switzerland because some of the people look Swiss, but it could be Italy or France. I'm not sure. It doesn't look like a very expensive restaurant. The people look as if they're very good friends.
OK and the second one. Well, I'm not sure about this photograph actually. Ummm. It's a busy self-service restaurant. There are people in a queue waiting to order food. They look as if they know each other. The man behind the counter looks smart. The restaurant could be in England or the USA, but I don't know.

Writing p.25

1 (suggested answer)
first paragraph ends: *I've been really busy*
second paragraph ends: *see it too*
third paragraph ends: *of Paris too*
fourth paragraph ends: *seeing?*

2 1 A   2 B   3 A   4 A   5 B   6 A

3 a sci fi   b romance   c comedy   d thriller   e horror
f musical

UNIT 4

Grammar 1 p.26

1 1 Who won the Eurovision Song Contest last year?
2 What did you do last weekend?
3 He didn't understand French very well the first time he went to Paris.
4 We all felt ill after the meal.

5 Mike threw the car keys and Tina caught them.
6 We bought Elena some perfume for her birthday.

2 1 A 2 A 3 B 4 B

3 1 saw, got
2 was fixing, was making, heard
3 was talking, came, asked
4 was dancing, walked
5 was trying, were digging

4 1 was studying 2 was working 3 liked 4 decided
5 chose 6 arrived 7 was waiting 8 was wearing
9 thought 10 took 11 enjoyed 12 were waiting
13 realised 14 didn't know 15 didn't have 16 said
17 felt 18 didn't have 19 explained 20 didn't mind

Grammar 2 p.27

1 1 didn't talk, had been
2 didn't understand, had failed
3 didn't watch, had stopped
4 had grown, recognised
5 had left, paid
6 saw, had just returned
7 had parked, walked
8 felt, hadn't ridden

2 1 knew, hadn't come 2 met, had (never) been
3 phoned, hadn't heard 4 borrowed, realised, had seen
5 got, had (already) found 6 spent, had (already) visited

3 1 I **was** so bored; I **realised** how late it was, my favourite
programme **had** already finished
2 We **waited**; we **got** a taxi; we **got** to the station, the
train **had already gone**
3 when we **got** to the checkout, André **realised** he didn't
have his wallet; while we **were waiting**; he **felt**
someone; We **realised** this person **had taken** the
wallet.

Vocabulary 1 p.29

1 1 B 2 C 3 B 4 C 5 A 6 C 7 A 8 B

2 1 chemistry 2 engineering 3 biology 4 medicine
5 law 6 psychology 7 economics 8 history
9 architecture 10 philosophy 11 physics

Vocabulary 2 p.30

1 1 beautifully, well 2 successful 3 good 4 badly
5 happily 6 noisy 7 seriously

2 1 noisily 2 successfully 3 happily 4 carefully
5 clearly 6 easily

3 1 well 2 fast 3 hard 4 well 5 hard 6 fast

Listening p.31

1 1 c 2 b 3 e 4 f 5 a 6 d

3 1 A 2 B 3 C 4 B 5 C 6 A

Tapescript

I had always wanted to be an actor. There was an
advertisement in the newspaper for a famous acting school
with a date for auditions and I decided to go along. There
were a lot of other people waiting outside. They were all very
nervous and some of them were walking up and down

talking to themselves. I asked a girl what they were doing
and she explained that there was a website about the acting
school. It told you that for the audition you had to learn a
speech from one of Shakespeare's plays. The people talking
to themselves were actually rehearsing their speeches. I
hadn't seen the website so of course I hadn't learnt a speech
but I thought I could probably remember the famous one
from Hamlet. You know! The one that begins: 'To be, or not
to be? That is the question…' Finally it was my turn. Inside
there was a small theatre. Two men and a woman were
sitting in the front row. They looked very bored and tired.
There was a girl on stage playing the part of Juliet from
Romeo and Juliet. Before she had finished her speech, one of
the men stopped her. She looked as if she was going to cry,
but she said 'thank you' and walked off. I stepped onto the
stage and said 'Hello, my name is Jonathan Davie and I'm
going to play Hamlet.' I wasn't feeling nervous and I started
off well 'To be, or not to be? That is the question.' Then I
heard the woman say very quietly 'Oh no! Not another one'.
I realised lots of the other people had used the same speech.
I felt really stupid. I said the next part of the line and then I
knew I had completely forgotten the rest of the speech. It
was terribly embarrassing. I explained that I hadn't seen the
website and they told me to go away and learn another
speech and to come back the next day. I went straight to the
library and borrowed The Complete Works of William
Shakespeare. I chose one of Romeo's speeches in the end.
I practised it and practised it until I knew it perfectly. I did my
audition the next day and I got into the acting school. One of
my classmates was the girl who had played Juliet. Her name
is Kate…

Writing p.32

1 1 A 2 B 3 A 4 B

2 Sample text:
One morning, I was watching some young people playing
a game of beach volleyball. One of the players, a young
girl, invited me to join the game. At first, when I started
playing, I served the ball into the net. I was very
embarrassed. Then the girl showed me how to serve
properly. I tried again and this time I made a great serve
and everyone cheered. Finally, at the end of the game,
everyone congratulated me and I felt very happy.

UNIT 5

Grammar 1 p.33

1 1 had a shower every morning 2 had enjoyed the
exhibition 3 would post the letter 4 could speak
Spanish 6 the following week 7 the day before/the
previous day 8 the month before/the previous month
9 the following year

2 1 she had bought a new jacket the week before.
2 he would be in London the following week.
3 she wanted to do a postgraduate course the following
year.
4 she could come the following Wednesday.
5 he hadn't watched television the night before.
6 he couldn't play the piano.

3 1 She **said** she …/She **told us** she …
2 ✓
3 ✓
4 Carla **told** us …
5 He **said** I could …

Grammar 2 p.34

1 1 why I liked him.
2 when he had started acting.
3 which films he had acted in.
4 when I had seen his last film.
5 where he lived.
6 who he was married to.

2 1 He asked me if I thought he was more attractive than Ben Affleck.
2 He asked me if I thought he was a good actor.
3 He asked me if I had enjoyed his latest film.
4 He asked me if Jennifer Aniston was in it too.
5 He asked me if I had seen the TV series *Friends*.
6 He asked me if I had seen any films starring Courtney Cox.
7 He asked me if I was going to the cinema that weekend.
8 He asked me if he could come with me.

Vocabulary 1 p.35

1 1 c 2 f 3 d 4 e 5 a

2 get over breaking up with Carlos
get through to the manager
get round a difficulty
get away with not handing in your homework

3 1 on with her neighbours.
2 away with not handing in his homework
3 through to the manager
4 difficulties/problems I had to get round
5 over breaking up with Carlos.

Vocabulary 2 p.36

1 get over   2 get away with   3 get round
4 get through to   5 get on with

Vocabulary 3 p.36

1 Photographs A and B should be ticked.

2 1 wavy, slim, moustache   2 tall, quite thin, well-built
3 blonde   4 curly, straight

3 1 medium height
2 slim
3 overweight
4 attractive
5 beard

Tapescript

Both these photographs are of couples. In the first photograph I think they are boyfriend and girlfriend. They seem to be in their twenties. The woman has dark wavy hair and the man is slim with a moustache. It looks like they are having a very good time. Perhaps it is the woman's birthday and they have gone out to dinner to celebrate.

In the second photograph we can see a couple in their garden. I think they look like a married couple. The woman is tall and quite thin but the man is quite well-built. They're with a little girl. She looks like their daughter because she is blonde and so are the man and woman. The little girl has got curly hair but the woman has straight hair.

Speaking

1 1 AP   2 D   3 DS   4 AC   5 D

3 1 I agree up to a point
2 That's right!
3 In my opinion …
4 I think …
5 I don't really agree.
6 I don't agree at all!

4 (suggested answers)
1 I think …
2 I don't agree at all!
3 That's right!
4 I don't really agree.
5 That's right!
6 I think … / In my opinion …
7 I agree up to a point but …

Tapescript

A: I think people spend too much money on their appearance.
B: I agree up to a point, but looking attractive is important.
C: That's right! Attractive people earn more money.
D: In my opinion, that's really unfair.
A: I think it shouldn't matter what someone looks like.
B: I don't really agree. It's important in some jobs.
C: Well, it shouldn't be.
D: I don't agree at all! Models and actors have to be attractive!

Writing p.38

1 1 Carlos couldn't find a job so he stayed at home and looked after the house.
2 Olivia wanted to stay at home with Carlos but they needed money.
3 She had to find a job so she started looking at the job advertisements in the newspaper.
4 She started working in an English school but/although the salary wasn't very good.
5 It was quite expensive living in France and / so they could only just get by.
6 Olivia made lots of friends, although her French wasn't very good.
7 She could understand it quite well although / but she couldn't speak very much.
8 Carlos spoke French fluently because he had studied it at university.
9 He didn't have many opportunities to speak it because he was at home all day.
10 He started to feel lonely so he joined the local drama club.

2 1 There was a disgusting smell coming from the kitchen.
2 She told him sternly that he would have to leave.

3 Where the frog had been before there was a handsome prince.

4 She was terrified when she saw the Big Friendly Giant.

5 When she saw her boyfriend in the street with another girl, she was furious.

6 She was heartbroken when she saw the Beast lying in the garden.

3 (suggested answer)

I had never believed in ghosts until that night in March. I was staying in an old castle. I woke up in the middle of the night because there was a disgusting smell in my room. I looked around to try and find where it was coming from and I saw a figure carrying its head under its arm. I was terrified, but I spoke to it very sternly and I told it to go away. It put its head on its shoulders, turned around and smiled at me. I realised it was a rather handsome ghost. Then it disappeared.

Next morning the man who owned the house was delighted when I told the story. He said it was the ghost of his great-great-great-grandfather, although no one had seen him for 100 years!

UNIT 6

Grammar 1 p.40

1 1 I'll wear   2 I think I'll finish   3 I think I'll order
4 I'll have

2 1 'm going to cook   2 are going to play
3 are going to get   4 are going to deliver

3 1 will   2 are going to   3 are going to   4 will
5 am going to

4 1 am going to   2 will   3 will   4 are going to
5 will   6 are you going to   7 will   8 'm going to
9 Are you going to   10 you are going to

Grammar 2 p.42

1 1 is having   2 leaves   3 begins, finishes/ends
4 is picking up

2 1 leaves   2 gets   3 am going   4 starts   5 arrive
6 Are you doing

Vocabulary p.42

1 1 at   2 on   3 of   4 from   5 with   6 of   7 to
8 to

2 1 What subjects are you good at?
2 Which member of your family are you most similar to/is most similar to you?
3 What kinds of music are you interested in?
4 What things are you worried about?
5 Which member of your family are you most different from/is most different from you?
6 What things are you most afraid of?

3 1 A   2 B   3 B   4 D   5 D   6 A   7 B   8 B   9 B   10 C

Reading p.44

1 a 3   b 5   c 1   d 6   e 3

2 1 B   2 A   3 C   4 A   5 D

3 1 loveable   2 frightening   3 anxious   4 impressive
5 uncomfortable   6 pleasant   7 appealing

4 1 appealing   2 uncomfortable   3 impressive
4 loveable   5 frightening   6 pleasant   7 anxious

Listening p.45

1 1, 4, 5 and 7 should be ticked

2 1 T   2 T   3 F   4 F   5 T   6 T   7 F

Tapescript

B = Bettina   A = Alberto

A: Did you see that article about the writer who spent a whole week without using any modern technology?

B: Why did he do that?

A: It was an experiment. If he wanted to make a phone call he had to use a public phone! Can you imagine that? And he wasn't even allowed to switch his computer on, so he couldn't look at his email messages or send any.

B: Well, I wouldn't find the phone part difficult but the other things might be hard.

A: So you still haven't got a mobile phone, Bettina. Incredible! But you'd find it really difficult if you couldn't even use the phone in your house.

B: Couldn't he use his home phone?

A: No, only public phones. And he had to do all his writing by hand or on an old typewriter. It took him ages because he kept making mistakes and having to start again. He was so used to being able to correct everything on the computer, you know, with the spelling and grammar check.

B: Yes that would be hard! How did he feel about not using his mobile?

A: Oh, he really hated it. He was late for all his appointments and he couldn't tell the people who were waiting for him that he was stuck in a traffic jam or whatever. And he really missed being able to read his messages and, well, just talking to people.

B: I think I'd miss email most.

A: He did too. He said it was really terrible. Also apparently he normally does a lot of research on the internet so when he needed information he didn't know what to do. In the end he went to a public library but it took him ages to find what he wanted.

B: So what was the point of the experiment?

A: Well, to show how dependent we've become on technology.

B: And has the man decided to stop using all these things?

A: No, I don't think so. He said that he was just really glad when the week was over and he could get back to normal life.

B: I would be too.

Writing p.46

1 across
1 asap
4 mon
6 etc

down
2 sat
3 pm
5 nb
6 eg

2 (suggested answers)
1 ~~Dear~~ Gianni
~~I am writing to tell you that I~~ have gone to ~~the~~ beach with ~~my sister~~ Elena. ~~I will be back this~~ ~~evening~~ **p.m.** Can you ~~please~~ water ~~the~~ plants?
~~Love~~
Carla
2 ~~Dear~~ Alex
~~How are you? Your friend~~ Marek phoned this ~~morning~~ **a.m.** ~~Would you please~~ phone him back **a.s.a.p.** on ~~this~~ tel. no.: 4596351.
~~All the best~~
Ania

3 (suggested answers)
1 Alba
Gone to Katie's house. Borrowed your backpack. Coming back Fri p.m.
Ana
2 Sam
Gone to gym. Will cook dinner when I get back. Can you get coffee and orange juice?
Ana

UNIT 7

Grammar 1 p.47

1 1 must send   2 must meet up   3 have to wear   4 has to write   5 have to take

2 1 You mustn't walk on the grass.
2 You mustn't feed the animals.
3 You mustn't park here.
4 You mustn't use a mobile phone.
5 You mustn't play football on the beach.

3 1 He says that I have to be home before 11 p.m.
2 The doctor says that I have to drink more water, especially when it's hot.
3 She says that I have to eat lots of fruit and vegetables.
4 The dentist says that I have to brush my teeth after every meal.
5 She says that I have to have a check-up every six months.

4 1 have to   2 don't have to   3 must   4 have to   5 must   6 must

Grammar 2 p.48

1 1 Can you lend   2 Can you slow down.
3 Could you phone   4 Can I try on   5 Could you/I close the window   6 Could you write   7 Could I get   8 Can you tell

2 1 Would you help me move these boxes, please?
2 Would you take me to Harcourt Avenue, please?
3 Would you tell the teacher that I am going to be late, please?
4 Would you feed my cats while I am away, please?
5 Would you mind telling me where you bought your t-shirt?
6 Would you be a bit quieter, please?

3 a 2   b 3   c 1   d no dialogue
(suggested answers)
1 Can I   2 I'm sorry,   3 can I   4 Yes, of course.
5 Could you   6 Sorry   7 Could I   8 Yes, of course.
9 Can you   10 I'm sorry.   11 can   12 No problem.

4 (suggested answer)
A: Could you tell me when the next train to Brighton leaves, please?
B: Yes, of course. The express train is at ten thirty and the slow train is at five past ten.
A: Can I have a return ticket for the express train, please?
B: Yes, of course. That's £18.50, please.

Vocabulary 1 p.50

1 tennis: court, net, umpire, racket
athletics: track
motor racing: track, crash helmet
football: pitch, captain
basketball: court, captain

2 1 spectators   2 final   3 driver   4 race   5 putting on   6 giving   7 Championships   8 game   9 referee   10 players

Vocabulary 2 p.51

1 1 b   2 d   3 e   4 c   5 a   6 f

2 1 C   2 A   3 B   4 C

3 1 A   2 C   3 B   4 A   5 B   6 B

Listening p.52

1 1 b   2 e   3 a   4 f   5 d   6 c

2 1 Chicago   2 older brother   3 10,000   4 surfing   5 legs   6 two months

Tapescript

I = Interviewer   S = Shannon

I: Have you always been interested in snow sports?
S: Well, my father encouraged me to try out lots of sports when I was growing up in Chicago and then in the town of Steamboat, Colorado. I guess I was pretty good at most of them. But once I'd tried snowboarding, I knew it was the one for me.
I: So how did you start?

S: Well, my older brother Sean was already snowboarding and I used to follow him and his friends around. I just wanted to learn everything I could. He was great! He never made me feel stupid even though I wasn't nearly as fast or as good at snowboarding as he was. I finished High School early so I could go on a snowboarding tour with him.

I: Where did you get the money to go on tour?

S: Our parents gave us each $10,000 and then we had to find our own financial support by getting sponsors.

I: Weren't your parents worried about a young girl doing such a dangerous sport?

S: Both my Mom and Dad are athletic and they know what it's like to compete. They've always encouraged me. They agree that young girls need to know that they can try different things and not be afraid of failing.

I: You obviously enjoy competing.

S: Yes but the competition part isn't as important as the fun! I keep it new and exciting by trying new things. My husband Dave and I spend our summers surfing. I love to be in the water. It's the best thing after a season of cold weather and sore legs! In snowboarding you mainly use your legs and in surfing it's mainly the upper part of your body, so it gives me a chance to recover and improve my balance skills at the same time.

I: It sounds as if you are on the move most of the year.

S: We are. We only spend about two months a year at home.

Speaking p.52

1 The boy

2 1 don't you   2 What about you?   3 do you like

3 (suggested answers)
I like swimming alone like that, don't you?
Jogging and skiing. What do you like?

Tapescript

J = Josue   N = Nadia

J: I think water aerobics would be a lot of fun, don't you?

N: I'm not sure. I've never tried it.

J: No, I haven't tried it either, but they seem to be having a great time jumping around in the water. It looks like a mixture of swimming and aerobics. I like aerobics and I love swimming. What about you?

N: I like swimming alone like that.

J: Yes, I like to swim alone sometimes too. What other kinds of exercises do you like?

N: Jogging and skiing.

Writing p.53

1 1 d   2 c   3 a   4 e   5 b

2 1 One of the most interesting places in my city is the old town. It was built in the sixteenth century and it is still there today. When you come here you must visit it.
   2 Most of the tourists who come here are English and they don't usually understand very much Spanish. My friend Jenny does though. She did a course at the University of Salamanca last year.

   3 I'm going to Venice, Florence, Pisa and Rome. If I have time I want to visit Naples too. Rosaria, the girl I met in Bristol last summer, lives there.
   4 'Watch out! You're going to drop those plates,' shouted my mother, but it was too late. I'd already dropped them.
   5 My cousin's favourite sport is basketball. She's got photos of players from the top teams all over her bedroom wall. She doesn't play basketball herself, though.

3 The inappropriate alternatives are:
Bye; How do you do?; What a surprise! I am looking forward to; Finally; Yours faithfully

UNIT 8

Grammar 1 p.54

1 1 I have seen all of the films that won Oscars.
   2 She has visited France, Italy and Spain.
   3 She hasn't travelled anywhere outside Europe.
   4 Have they (ever) tried snowboarding?
   5 Have you (ever) eaten frogs' legs?
   6 Have you (ever) ridden a camel or an elephant?

2 1 I've never been surfing myself
   2 I have never tried it either.
   3 I've already bought a surfboard.
   4 if you haven't had any lessons yet?
   5 I've already talked to lots of surfers
   6 Have you already bought a wetsuit?
   7 It hasn't ever seemed particularly cold to me.

3 1 already   2 never   3 yet   4 already   5 never   6 yet
   7 just   8 yet, yet, just

4 1 did you eat   2 had   3 Did you like   4 have eaten
   5 have ever eaten   6 ate

5 1 haven't written   2 have already done   3 have taken
   4 have been   5 went   6 have never seen
   7 haven't been   8 has managed

Grammar 2 p.56

1 1 I haven't seen her for a couple of weeks.
   2 She has been away on holiday since the beginning of August.
   3 How long has Bea lived in Madrid?
   4 She has lived there since the beginning of 2002.
   5 Have you ever shared a flat with her?
   6 We (have) only shared a flat for a month.
   7 We have known each other for much longer.
   8 I have met her family and her boyfriend.

2 1 have visited   2 have stopped   3 have learnt
   4 have done   5 has said   6 have had

3 1 have you lived in Verona?
   2 seen Simon since August.
   3 known Simon for ten years.
   4 been to Greece three times.
   5 ever been to Europe before?

Vocabulary 1 p.57

1 a roof   b chimney   c garage   d path   e front door
f fence   g gate   h front garden   i drive

2 1 in the garage, on the corner of my street, outside my
friend's house
2 in a block of flats, on the ground floor, on a boat
3 along the path, next to the gate, in the front garden

Vocabulary 2 p.57

I'm very **tired**; this can be a bit **depressing**; which I found
absolutely **fascinating**; I won't be at all **surprised**

Reading p.58

1 1 Sunny   2 Jeffrey   3 Mary   4 Jeffrey
5 Sunny and Jeffrey

2 1 A   2 B   3 D   4 C   5 D   6 D

3 1 marinas   2 polluted   3 confident   4 overcrowded
5 move on / sail off   6 get on with   7 ahead of

Writing p.59

1 1 i   2 b   3 c   4 e   5 h   6 g   7 f   8 a   9 d

2 Paragraph 1: i, b
Paragraph 2: c, e
Paragraph 3: h, g, f
Paragraph 4, a, d

3 1 although   2 However   3 On the other hand
4 Although   5 However

4 (suggested answers)
1 The trains were very expensive, but they were very dirty
and didn't run on time.
2 We left for the airport in plenty of time, however / but
we still missed the plane.
3 Although there is a very efficient bus service on the
island we chose to hire a car.
4 The streets were quite crowded during the day. On the
other hand, there was no nightlife at all that we could
find.
5 The food in the seaside restaurants is excellent,
however / but the service is very poor.

5 (suggested answer)
Dear Fiodr
Thank you so much for your letter. I am pleased to hear
about your new girlfriend, **although** it's sad that things
didn't work out between you and Tanya.
The house looks wonderful now. It took us a very long
time to finish all the decorating, **but** it was worth all the
effort! Sometimes I think we should have used a
professional decorator – it would have saved us so much
work. **On the other hand**, it would have cost us a lot
more money!
Ulrike has started school now. She was nervous about her
first day, **although** she was very excited to be starting at
'proper' school. I felt a little sad saying goodbye to her.
However, I'm enjoying the extra free time at home.

UNIT 9

Grammar 1 p.61

1 1 d   2 f   3 e   4 c   5 b

2 1 which   2 whose   3 who   4 where   5 when

3 1 La Gomera is one of the places where they use whistling
language.
2 It is also where we go for our holidays.
3 August is the month when we usually go there.
4 Stelios is the Greek boy who I met there last summer.
5 He is the one whose brother plays for Newcastle United.
6 Newcastle United were not the team that won the
championship.

4 2, 4, 5 and 7 should be ticked.

Grammar 2

1 1 ND   2 ND   3 D   4 D   5 ND   6 D

2 1 To celebrate her birthday, which is next week, we are all
going out for a pizza.
2 Pizzeria Da Canio, where we went for my birthday last
year as well, is not very expensive.
3 In September, when Clara will be in Dublin, I might go
and visit her.
4 The family she is going to stay with, who have twin
daughters called Maeve and Sinead, is really nice.
5 Trinity College, Dublin, where Maeve and Sinead are
studying, has a special course for students of English as
a foreign language.
6 At Christmas, when Clara goes back to Barcelona,
Maeve and Sinead are going to organise a big farewell
party for her.

3 1 His English, which he had learnt from listening to songs,
was not very good when he arrived in the United States.
2 *Some Like it Hot*, which starred Marilyn Monroe, is one
of his best-known films.
3 Billy Wilder shared a room with an actor called Peter
Laurie, who was also trying to find work.
4 Eventually Peter Laurie, who was in the film *Casablanca*,
became very famous.
5 By 2002, when Billy Wilder died, he had written more
than seventy films.

Vocabulary 1 p.64

1 whispering   2 sneezed   3 ringing   4 shouting
5 whistling   6 screaming   7 bang   8 slammed

Vocabulary 2 p.64

1 1 get through to   2 speak up   3 shut up   4 making up
5 told (me) off   6 catches on   7 look (it) up

2 1 C   2 A   3 C   4 A   5 B

3 1 making (it) up   2 look (them) up   3 shut up
4 speak up   5 catches on   6 told me off

Reading p.65

1 1 Italian   2 Spanish   3 French   4 Japanese

2 1 Clare, Tom   2 Liam   3 Tom   4 Janna   5 Janna
6 Janna, Tom   7 Liam, Tom   8 Clare

Speaking p.66

1 She compares photographs 2 and 3.

2 1 both   2 In the first one   3 seems to be
4 Although, are similar

3 1 I mean   2 what it's called   3 sorry
4 Things that, to listen

4 Both photographs are about learning languages.
In the first one I can see some students in a language
laboratory. They are wearing … I'm not sure what it's
called in English, but I think it might be 'headphones'. The
students are listening to a cassette or perhaps to their
instructor.
In the other photograph I can see a chimpanzee. It seems
to be learning sign language because the instructor is
making a sign.
Although they are quite different, the two photographs
are similar because both the chimpanzee and the students
are listening carefully.

Tapescript

Well, both these photographs are about communication. In
the first one I can see a person reading a book, but the book
is writing … I mean written … in a special language. I'm not
sure what it's called in English but in my language we call it
Braille. People who can't see … I mean blind people can read
these books. They feel the letters with their fingers.
The other photograph seems to be an important international
meeting. It could be the Nations … sorry, the United Nations,
but I'm not sure. Some of the people are wearing … what's
the word … things that you put on your ears to listen.
Because all the people at the meeting speak different
languages there are translators. They listen to what the
people say and translate it into another language. Although
they are quite different, the two photographs are similar
because they both show people communicating in special
ways.

Writing p.67

1 1✓ 2✓ 3✗ 4✗ 5✓ 6✓ 7✗ 8✓ 9✗

2 A

3 (suggested answer)
As well as that, you learn about another culture.
In addition, it will be easy to get English books, records
and videos, which you can use when you go back to your
country.

UNIT 10

Grammar 1 p.68

1 1 If I have a basketball match, I get up much earlier.
2 If it's a sunny morning, I walk to the sports club.
3 If it's raining, my sister drives me.
4 If she's not busy, she stays to watch the match.
5 If our team wins, we all go out for lunch to celebrate.

2 1 had, would live   2 won't be, drive   3 have, drink
4 would live, got   5 doesn't drink, feels
6 will be, forget

3 1 met   2 are   3 would you feel   4 you don't have
5 would you do   6 will happen

4 a 6 b 0 c 5 d 2 e 3 f 4 g 1

Grammar 2 p.70

1 1 f 2 a 3 e 4 c 5 d

2 1 hadn't answered, wouldn't have met
2 would have gone back, hadn't started
3 would have married, hadn't married
4 had married, would have had
5 had been, would have called
6 would have let, had been
7 would have been, hadn't answered

3 1 If I hadn't got up late, I would have been able to go to
basketball training.
2 If she had looked at the weather forecast, she would
have known it was going to rain all day.
3 If he hadn't stayed up late, he wouldn't have been tired
in the exam.
4 If he hadn't promised to change, I wouldn't have
decided to come back.
5 If I had listened to my friend's advice, I wouldn't
have bought a big dog.
6 If you had run as fast as I did last time, you would have
won the race.

4 1 are not too busy, we visit my aunt on Saturdays.
2 hadn't forgotten my keys last night, I wouldn't have
broken a window to get in.
3 practises, her tennis will improve.
4 hurries, she will catch the train.
5 'm depressed, I eat chocolate.
6 had a bicycle, he wouldn't walk/would cycle to school.

Vocabulary 1 p.71

1 1 f 2 d 3 a 4 c 5 g 6 b 7 e

2 1 over 100 kilometres   2 32   3 16–18 hours
4 1939   5 22 kilos   6 7 centimetres tall   7 37%

3 1 How long   2 What percentage   3 How long
4 how much you weighed   5 What's the fastest speed
6 What's the population   7 How far

Vocabulary 2 p.72

1 1 b 2 c 3 a 4 f 5 d 6 e

2 1 Honestly   2 Anyway   3 You know   4 Suddenly
5 Can you believe it?   6 Anyway   7 In the end

Listening p.72

1 Speaker 1: dog   Speaker 2: fish   Speaker 3: bird
Speaker 4: rabbits

2 1 F 2 F 3 T 4 T 5 F 6 F 7 T 8 F 9 T 10 F

Tapescript

Speaker 1
I had never really thought about getting a pet but one day
there was this poor little thing sitting outside the library at
college. She looked terrible. It was very cold and she was
shaking. She was also very thin and had a cut on her paw.
I just couldn't bear it. I mean, what had she done to deserve

this? In the end, I took her home. We call her Lucky and she's just like another member of the family now. Honestly, I can't understand why she was abandoned in the first place. She's very obedient and always comes when you call her.

Speaker 2

We got Freddie about four years ago. He is a beautiful blue/black colour and he has a long black tail and black fins. We got a special tank for him, and filled it with plants and different coloured stones. The tank also has a pump which keeps the water clean and oxygenated. But we would sometimes wonder if he was lonely, swimming around in his tank all by himself. So, last year, we bought a companion for him – Jimmie. Jimmie is a standard gold colour. They ignore each other a lot of the time, but I think that Freddie must be happier now that he has a friend in his tank.

Speaker 3

Tweety, was a real character. We used to let him fly around the house but it was never very difficult to get him to go back into his cage. He'd get tired and go back of his own accord or you could put a lettuce leaf inside and he'd fly back in to eat it. Anyway, one day he had been hopping around in the living room all afternoon looking at himself in the mirror from time to time. I was working but when I went to try to get him back into the cage, I couldn't find him. I looked everywhere. I was really worried and was beginning to think he'd got out when something made me look behind the mirror. Can you believe it? There he was …sound asleep.

Speaker 4

I'd offered to look after my friends' house while they were away on holiday. I was living just round the corner so it wasn't difficult for me to go round once a day and check that everything was OK. The only hard part was that they had two pet rabbits, Harry and Bill. They had a special cage and an area with a fence where they could hop about. One day they were in there together when Harry suddenly jumped over the fence. I didn't know he was able to jump that high so it was a real shock. It took me about ten minutes to catch him and put him back. Then…can you believe it?…Bill jumped out!

Speaking p.73

1 1 e 2 b 3 f 4 d 5 a

2 b 4 c 1 d 6 e 3 f 5 g 7 h 8

3 (suggested answer)
1 Why don't we get a dog? Dogs are fun to play with.
2 Mmm, that's a good suggestion, but a dog would be too difficult to look after in a flat.
3 I agree, and dogs are difficult to train too.
4 OK, well what about a cat? Cats are very clean and you don't have to take them for walks.
5 Yes, that's a good idea. I agree. Cats are easy to look after, so let's get a cat.

Writing p.74

1 Report B

2 <u>Here are some things you should think about</u> if you're going to buy a pet. <u>Let's start with</u> dogs. They're <u>OK</u>. <u>I mean</u>, they're friendly and fun to play with but <u>who's going to take a dog for a walk a couple of times a day</u>? <u>Not me, that's for sure</u>. The dog will get very bored and fat. He will bark a lot. The neighbours will complain. <u>What</u>

<u>about cats</u>? <u>Great</u>, but they don't like being moved. If you go on holiday you can't take them with you. You have to get a friend to come and give them their food. <u>What about birds</u>? I think they're a fantastic idea because they don't cost very much and you can move them easily. They make really good pets. <u>You know</u>, I think birds are the best choice.

3 Exotic animals are fascinating, <u>so</u> people think they will be good pets.
<u>Consequently</u>, they get ill and sometimes even die.
… the animals are sometimes brought here illegally <u>so</u> if we buy them, we help the people who break the law …

UNIT 11

Grammar 1 p.76

1 1 Tim's car is newer than Tina's car. Tina's car isn't as new as Tim's car. Tina's car is less new than Tim's.
2 Tim's car is more comfortable than Tina's car. Tina's car isn't as comfortable as Tim's car. Tina's car is less comfortable than Tim's.
3 Tim's car is faster than Tina's car. Tina's car isn't as fast as Tim's car. Tina's car is less fast than Tim's.
4 Tina's car is noisier than Tim's car. Tim's car isn't as noisy as Tina's car. Tim's car is less noisy than Tina's.
5 Tim's car is more expensive than Tina's car. Tina's car isn't as expensive as Tim's car. Tina's car is less expensive than Tim's.

2 ~~biger~~ – bigger
~~thiner~~ – thinner
~~widder~~ – wider
~~cheapper~~ – cheaper

3 1 more difficult 2 more exciting 3 most enjoyable
4 happier 5 more boring

4 1 more 2 worst 3 more 4 than 5 less 6 most
7 less 8 than

Grammar 2 p.77

1 1 Why don't you go 2 you should ask 3 why don't you buy 3 You should borrow

2 1 shouldn't go, should go 2 shouldn't ask, should ask 3 shouldn't buy, should get 4 shouldn't borrow (money), should get

3 1 you ought/it would be better 2 should get
3 shouldn't leave 4 don't you try

4 1 you should ~~to~~ buy 2 Why **don't you** 3 shouldn**'t**
4 ought **to** go 5 shouldn't ~~to~~ worry

5 1 b 2 c 3 e 4 d 5 a

Vocabulary 1 p.78

1 waiter 4, private dectective 2, window cleaner 3, swimming instructor 1

2 1 well paid 2 stressful 3 good with numbers
4 have a good sense of humour 5 imaginative
6 curious 7 dangerous 8 brave 9 a good head for heights 10 fit 11 dangerous 12 good with people
13 patient

3 Text A: waiter Text B: cartoonist Text C: private detective Text D: window cleaner Text E: swimming instructor

Vocabulary 2 p.79

1 torch, bandage, mirror, blanket, spade, rope, aspirin, phone, matches, water

2 1 the bottle of water
2 is the most important thing
3 to attract attention
4 we ought to take
5 light a fire
6 why don't we take the
7 protect ourselves

Tapescript

L = Lucy   LK = Luke

Here are some things you might want to take on a camping trip in the mountains in case of an emergency. Decide between you which five items are most important.

L: Well, I think we should definitely take the bottle of water. It's very easy to get dehydrated, even in the mountains.
LK: Yes but not if there's snow or ice. I think the bandage is the most important thing. It would be useful for stopping the bleeding if one of us had a cut and we could also use it for other injuries.
L: OK. I agree. What about the torch?
LK: The batteries might run out, so I think we ought to take the mirror as well. We can use it to attract attention.
L: Yes, that's a good idea. I don't think the phone is very important, do you?
LK: No, not in the mountains, it wouldn't work, but I do think we ought to take the thermal blanket.
L: Yes if we have to spend a night in the open it could be very important. But we could take the matches too so that we can light a fire.
LK: Mmm. The trouble is matches get wet. We can always use the mirror to light a fire.
L: Yes, that's true. We can only have one more thing, so why don't we take the spade? We could dig a hole in the snow if we need to and protect ourselves from the cold.
LK: OK. So, we'll take the bandage, the torch, the mirror, the thermal blanket and the spade.

Reading p.80

1 a the shore   b boogie board   c an alligator

2 No.

3 1 C   2 C   3 A   4 A

4 a panicking   b drifting   c recovering   d mangled   e frantically

Writing p.81

1 1 F 2 I 3 I 4 F 5 I 6 F 7 I 8 I 9 F 10 F 11 I 12 I 13 F

2 Formal letter: 13, 9, 1, 6, 4, 10
Informal letter: 3, 7, 8, 2, 5, 11, 12

3 I wanted to tell you about something really terrifying that happened to a friend of mine a couple of weeks ago. ~~His name is James and I met him last summer when we were on holiday in Sardinia. Anyway,~~ He was on his ~~new purple and yellow, fibreglass~~ surfboard at a beach near here when suddenly he saw a ~~grey, black and white~~ shark ~~with big sharp, white teeth~~ swimming towards him. He was really terrified but luckily, he had read an article about sharks in a magazine ~~called 'Surf the Globe'~~ the day before. The article~~, which was written by someone called Lana Beachworth,~~ said that the best thing to do if a shark swims towards you is to hit it. Unfortunately, my friend didn't have anything to hit the shark with so he had to use his hand. Can you believe it? He punched the shark on the nose. In the end, it swam away and my friend was able to paddle back to shore. ~~This took him about five minutes.~~ He was shaking when he came out of the ~~clear blue~~ water.

Well, that's my main piece of news. Apart from going to the beach, I'm studying a lot for my exams ~~in mathematics, chemistry, geography and English~~ and looking forward to coming home for the holidays. Will you be around in August? Write and let me know.

UNIT 12

Grammar 1 p.82

1 1 My mother could ~~to~~ speak Chinese when she was young.
2 Were you able **to** go to the bank at lunchtime?
3 I **can't** see you today.
6 We **can't** afford to buy a new car.
8 Can you ~~be able to~~ help me with this exercise?

2 1 Will (you) be able to afford
2 Will (you) be able to borrow
3 Will (you) be able to get
4 Will (you) be able to drive

3 1 ✓ 2 ~~could~~ 3 ~~could~~ 4 ~~could~~ 5 ✓

4 1 C 2 A 3 B 4 A 5 A 6 A

Grammar 2 p.83

1 1 Yes, we always used to go to a guesthouse on the coast for two weeks.
2 Did you always use to go at the same time?
3 Yes, and we always used to see the same people.
4 What did you use to enjoy most about your holiday?
5 The only thing we <u>didn't</u> use to enjoy was the food.

2 1 Tina used to be my closest friend.
2 We used to meet up every day.
3 We used to go to a café, have coffee and talk.
4 Tina used to tell very funny stories.
5 She used to work in a big department store.
6 Princess Diana used to be a customer there.
7 She used to wear beautiful clothes.

3 1 People used to ride horses.
2 They didn't use to have electric lighting.
3 They didn't use to have mobile phones.
4 The women used to wear long dresses.
5 They didn't use to wear jeans.

Vocabulary 1 p.85

1 1 remember   2 forgotten   3 Remind   4 unforgettable
5 memorised   6 forget   7 reminder   8 forgetful
9 remember   10 forget

2 1 memorise   2 forgetful   3 reminder   4 unforgettable

3 1 g   2 d   3 b   4 a   5 f   6 c   7 e

Vocabulary 2 p.86

1 1 impossible   2 illegible   3 unfriendly
4 impatient   5 invisible   6 irresponsible
7 dishonest   8 uncomfortable

2 1 impossible   2 impatient   3 invisible   4 uncomfortable
5 dishonest   6 irresponsible   7 illegible   8 unfriendly

Reading p.86

1 Title A

2 1 e   2 d   3 f   4 c   5 a   6 b

3 a bump   b desire   c shivering   d recall   e rare

Listening p.87

1 A: 7, 10   B: 1, 6   C: 4, 8   D: 3, 9   E: 2, 5

2 Speaker 1: D   Speaker 2: B   Speaker 3: E   Speaker 4: A

3 Speaker 1: E   Speaker 2: C   Speaker 3: B   Speaker 4: A

Tapescript

Speaker 1
I remember hearing footsteps in the street coming up behind me. I felt quite anxious, and stressed, I was sure that someone was following me. Then suddenly someone tapped me on the shoulder. I turned round, terrified, and there was a young man looking at me. 'You're gorgeous!' he said and put a piece of paper and a red rose into my hand. Then he ran off down the street. He'd written his name and phone number on the piece of paper. I had a boyfriend at the time so I threw the number away. Now I can't even remember what he looked like.

Speaker 2
I was reading a magazine in the kitchen and listening to some music when the telephone rang. My girlfriend answered it. I couldn't hear what she was saying, but then she suddenly ran into the kitchen and shouted, 'You've won a motorcycle!' I'd entered a competition months earlier. I had to answer some really easy questions – I can't remember what they were now. I was absolutely thrilled – I'd never won anything before.

Speaker 3
I remember that my sister and I weren't allowed to go and see Mum in the hospital. It was against hospital regulations but I can't remember why. Anyway, we were really disappointed but Dad brought us a photo of little Michael so we could see him. We were so excited when Mum finally brought him home. We kept arguing about who would get to help Dad bath him and put him to bed. It's incredible to think that he was ever that small. He's almost two metres tall now.

Speaker 4
I came home from work very late and immediately I could see that Nick looked annoyed about something. When I asked him if anything was the matter he just said 'No' and walked out of the room. He'd cooked this really amazing meal … it must have taken hours and there were flowers and candles. 'What's the special occasion?' I asked. 'Our fifth wedding anniversary', he said. I've never felt so terrible in my life. Even though he'd mentioned it a few days before I'd completely forgotten about it.

Speaking p.88

1 The speaker describes photograph 1.

2 1 may be, not sure   2 obviously
3 looks like   4 is smiling   5 I would enjoy

3 1 outside   2 on   3 covered   4 better   5 prefer   6 sea

Tapescript

This photograph shows a family having a picnic somewhere out in the countryside. It may be the beach – I'm not sure, but it's obviously a hot day because they're all wearing summer clothes. It looks like a father, a mother and two children, a boy aged about 7 and a girl aged about 5. There's a blanket spread out on the ground and a couple of baskets and everyone is smiling and looking very happy. I think I would enjoy this kind of picnic. It looks very informal and relaxed.

Writing p.88

1 1 B, C   2 A, C   3 A, C   4 A, B

2 ~~bussy~~ – busy
~~forgoten~~ – forgotten
~~terible~~ – terrible
~~wining~~ – winning
~~where had I~~ – where I had
~~Mum would have already washed~~ – Mum had already washed
~~I was rushing out~~ – I rushed out

UNIT 13

Grammar 1

1 1 Paula likes cooking but she doesn't like washing up.
2 Paula likes surfing but she doesn't like skiing.
3 Paula likes swimming but she doesn't like mountain biking.
4 Paula likes visiting museums but she doesn't like visiting art galleries.
5 Paula likes watching horror films but she doesn't like watching romantic films.

2 1 likes   2 would like   3 doesn't like   4 would like
5 would like   6 doesn't like, would like, likes

3 1 Yes, but I would like to see New Zealand too.
2 My friend would like to study in Australia.
3 Would her parents like her to do that too?
4 No, they wouldn't like her to be so far from home.
5 They would like her to study in Europe.

4 1 I **would** like to visit   2 ✓   3 ✓
4 **Would** you like information   5 ✓   6 I **like** looking

5 1 don't look like   2 taste like   3 smells like
4 sounds like   5 sounds like

Grammar 2 p.91

1 1 do   2 can   3 would   4 have   5 did

2 1 can   2 have   3 will   4 am

3 1 wouldn't   2 'm not   3 haven't   4 isn't   5 didn't
6 can   7 do   8 did

4 1 I can.   2 I will.   3 I do.   4 I did.   5 I am.

Vocabulary 1 p.92

1 1 continent, desert   2 oceans   3 Forest   4 island,
mountain   5 Lake, lakes   6 river

2 1 volcano – b   2 lake – e   3 waterfall – c
4 wood – f   5 beach – a   6 cliff – d

3 1 beaches   2 cliff   3 volcano   4 waterfall   5 lake
6 wood

Vocabulary 2 p.93

1 1 crowded   2 duty free   3 nightlife   4 guidebook
5 flight   6 tube   7 film   8 souvenir

2 1 film   2 duty free   3 flight   4 guidebook   5 tube
6 nightlife   7 crowded   8 souvenirs

Listening p.94

1 The following pictures should be ticked: a, b, d, e, f

2 1 $249   2 $14   3 100   4 one and a half hours
5 20 kilometres   6 Wednesday   7 9 o'clock in the
evening

3 1 S   2 D   3 S   4 D   5 S   6 S

Tapescript

Queenstown is Adventure town. There are lots of different
things to do.
Try the Southern hemisphere's highest bungy jump. Our
jumps are the oldest and the safest. Prices include full
instructions and equipment. Single jumps are $159 with
discounts if you want to repeat the same jump again. You
might enjoy it so much that you want to try all three jumps.
You save money if you do all three. It's only $249.
If bungee jumping is a little too adventurous for you, why not
take the gondola ride 450 metres above Queenstown to
enjoy the fantastic views of Lake Wakatipu below. $14 buys
you a trip on the gondola and $44 the trip plus lunch in our
restaurant.
Queenstown is also the place to relax and enjoy the natural
beauty of the mountains. A great way to see them is from
the lake aboard the TSS Earnslaw, a 100-year-old steamboat.
This is a favourite with young and old alike. There are regular
departures at 12.00, 2.00 and 4.00 pm and the trip takes
one and a half hours.
And if it's history that interests you most then take a short
trip to Arrowtown. It's only 20 kilometres away and has one
of the best historical museums in New Zealand. You can visit

the Lake District Museum every day except Sundays. It's open
from 10 in the morning till 5 except on Wednesday, when it's
closed in the afternoon. The town itself is full of historical
interest. Charming 19th century buildings line the main
street, many of them now elegant shops and restaurants.
When the autumn leaves have fallen, it's time to head for the
snow. The Queenstown area offers great runs for skiers and
snowboarders of all levels. Coronet Peak is New Zealand's
only night skiing area. Try it from 9 o'clock every evening.

Writing p.95

1 1 e   2 a   3 d   4 c   5 b

2 Plan A

3 A 2   B 1

4 ~~describbing~~ – describing
~~unforgetable~~ unforgettable
~~diner~~ dinner
~~lattest~~ latest
~~equippment~~ equipment
~~visitted~~ visited

UNIT 14

Grammar 1 p.96

1 1 looks   2 much   3 are   4 is   5 a   6 a   7 isn't
8 is   9 many   10 is   11 is   12 some   13 some   14 is
15 come   16 say   17 good   18 some   19 advice
20 traffic   21 is

2 1 an   2 -   3 -   4 -   5 a   6 a   7 a   8 -   9 -   10 -

Grammar 2 p.97

1 1 a bicycle   2 a handsome prince   3 a walk   4 a frog
5 a kiss   6 a handsome prince   7 a bicycle

2 1 He tried to comfort the princess.
2 They started walking back to the castle together.
3 On the path they saw the frog.
4 'Look, there's the frog!' said the princess.
5 'You granted the wrong wish!' said the princess to the
frog.
6 'Where's the bicycle I wished for?' said the princess.
7 'Do you want a bicycle or the prince?' asked the frog.
8 'I want to keep the prince and have a bicycle as well!'
said the princess.

3 1 ✓   2 She's from ~~the~~ Peru.   3 ✓   4 We did a lot of
shopping in ~~the~~ Oxford Street.   5 ✓   6 I got my brother
a huge block of ~~the~~ chocolate.

Vocabulary 1 p.98

1 1 A   2 B   3 B   4 A   5 B   6 B   7 A   8 A

Vocabulary 2 p.99

1 1 e   2 f   3 b   4 g   5 d   6 c   7 h   8 a

2 1 takes after   2 took over/took on   3 taking a few days
off   4 take on   5 take up   6 take it in

126

Speaking p.99

1 Discussion 1.

2 a 1 b 2 c 1 d 5 e 3 f 5 g 4 h 1 i 4 j 5
k 3

Tapescript

N = Nikos   F = Fatima

Discussion 1

N: In my town we had a 'My town without my car' day. In my opinion, making people leave their cars at home is a really good idea. People can understand that they don't always need a car.

F: That's right. We had that day in my town too. A lot of people complained about it but I think it was a success. Ummm We have to sort out our rubbish like that. Do you think that would work where you live?

N: No, not really. People are very lazy. They don't want to have to decide what kind of rubbish to put in each bin.

F: Maybe they would need time to get used to it. After a couple of months they wouldn't mind so much, do you agree?

N: I'm not sure. Sometimes I think people are just selfish.

F: Yes, but I think the supermarket campaign would work well, don't you?

N: Well, it depends. People often go to the supermarket after work so they don't want to carry a basket with them all day. And the beach cleaning. A lot of people say it's not their responsibility to clean the beach. What do you think?

F: I don't agree at all!

N: No, I think we all enjoy the beach so we should all help keep it clean!

K = Karina   G = Gustavo

Discussion 2

K: We've had most of these campaigns in my town. They were all successful.

G: In my town we have not had these campaigns. The first one would not work because people don't like to touch dirty things. The government should clean the beaches. The second one would not work because people like their cars very much and to even go one day without your car would be horrible to them The third one is possible. The fourth one is not good for the same reason as I gave about the first.

K: Every day we go to the supermarket and we take a basket. We put everything in the basket after we pay. We don't have any plastic bags at home and we don't need them because we put…sort out all our rubbish. Ummm. I would help to clean the beach. Umm…I ride a bicycle and so do my parents. We've got a car but we only use it at weekends to do the shopping.

Reading p.100

1 a 1 b 4 c 2 d 0 e 3

2 1 B 2 A 3 D 4 C

3 1 evidence 2 destiny 3 telescope 4 subscribed
5 admit

Writing p.101

1 Plan A

2 1 f 2 d, e 3 b 4 a, c

3 a First of all b In the afternoon c as well

4 1 there 2 I'd like 3 get something 4 it's raining
5 ones

UNIT 15

Grammar 1 p.103

1 1 are produced 2 is performed 3 is served 4 are sold

2 1 your shoes are being polished 2 your shirt is being ironed 3 your breakfast is being prepared 4 Fido is being walked

3 1 was designed 2 were imported 3 was painted
4 was sold

Grammar 2 p.105

1 1 has his breakfast cooked 2 has his shoes polished
3 has his car serviced 4 has his bed made

2 1 He couldn't have his breakfast cooked. He had to cook it himself.
2 He couldn't have his shoes polished. He had to polish them himself.
3 He couldn't have his bed made. He had to make it himself.
4 He couldn't have his car serviced. He had to service it himself.

3 1 did you have it serviced/fixed 2 don't you have it delivered 3 did you have it made 4 don't you have it repaired

4 1 having **her windows cleaned** 2 **had** his wallet stolen
3 **having my computer repaired** 4 **don't we**

Vocabulary 1 p.106

1 consumers 2 products 3 market 4 research
5 logo 6 brand 7 advertisements 8 company

Vocabulary 2 p.106

1 a cook, a vegetarian, a dessert, raw vegetables

2 1 cooker 2 baking 3 roast 4 vegetarians 5 desserts
6 sweet 7 fattening 8 fried 9 raw

Listening p.107

1 1 e 2 d 3 a 4 b 5 c

2 1 B 2 B 3 A 4 C 5 B

Tapescript

Extract 1

A: Well, the results of the tests make it absolutely clear. You'll have to cut out dairy products completely.

B: What? Everything? You mean cheese and yoghurt and butter …?

A: Yes, I'm afraid so. And milk. You'll have to try a substitute like soya milk for tea and coffee if you really can't drink them black.

Extract 2

A: What's the food like in your family?

B: It's great! Every morning we have cornflakes and toast and sometimes bacon and eggs. The only problem is that we have the evening meal very early. Often I am very hungry in the night. And the food where you're staying? How is it?

A: Oh, the Wilsons lived in France for a long time, so they prepare a lot of typically French dishes. It's just like home.

Extract 3

A: Mobile Burgers. Simon speaking. Can I help you?

B: Yes, I'd like a double cheese burger, no onion.

A: Anything with that?

B: Oh yeah. And some chips and a chocolate milkshake.

A: What size chips? Small, medium or large?

B: Oh actually I don't think I'll have the chips.

A: OK. Address?

B: 21 Walker Street.

A: Fine. We'll be round in 15 minutes.

Extract 4

So if you don't have a microwave you heat your coconut oil in a deep pot like this one until it's smoking slightly. It's good and hot now, I think. Throw your corn into the pot and put the lid on firmly, like this. Then turn the heat off under the pan and enjoy the sound of that corn popping! There it goes!

Extract 5

Right. I hear that some people have been taking food and drinks into the computer room. This is absolutely not...I repeat not...allowed. It's valuable equipment and it can be damaged very easily. A major problem was caused by someone spilling a bottle of water the other day...so no food and no liquids or the room will be closed unless a teacher is there to supervise.

Speaking p.108

1 1 b 2 e 3 f 4 d 5 c 6 a

Tapescript

E = Evangelina   T = Thomas

E: What do you think?

T: I think it would be a really good idea to serve hot soup in the winter.

E: Well, it depends...One problem is that there isn't anywhere to sit down and eat it.

T: I'm sure you're right but...perhaps they could put in some tables and chairs. They should sell crisps, chocolate and cakes, though.

E: Don't you think they're all a bit fattening?

T: I agree they're fattening up to a point...but not if you don't eat them all the time.

E: Salads are a good idea, aren't they?

T: I think you're right. Most people like salads. They'll have to sell chewing gum and cigarettes.

E: I don't agree at all. In my opinion chewing gum is really disgusting and I don't think people should be encouraged to smoke either.

Writing p.109

1 Yes

2 B

3 1 b 2 g 3 h 4 e 5 i 6 f 7 c 8 a